Intermodal Transportation

– The Whole Story

by David R. McKenzie
Mark C. North
Daniel S. Smith

Jolene,
I wish you much
success with the
FRA

Regards
Dave McKenzie

Simmons-Boardman Books, Inc.
1809 Capitol Avenue, Omaha, NE 68102

McK = Personal
Binder #71
Q & D Inc
SF, CA

Cover design by Apple Juice Group, Chicago

First Edition, First Printing, August 1989

Library of Congress Catalog Card Number: 89-061911
ISBN: 0-911382-09-7

FOREWORD

In writing *Intermodal Transportation – The Whole story*, we have attempted to describe the way in which intermodal transportation – the shipment of containerized cargo by more than one mode – has begun to revolutionize the movement of goods throughout the United States. Although some of our discussions mention intermodal activities in Canada and elsewhere, and also touch on the operations of container ships in international trade, the primary focus of the book is on surface intermodal transportation as it functions within the United States.

Certainly, the 1992 removal of trade barriers among the 12 members of the European Community will have profound impacts on transportation services in Europe that will, no doubt, spill over to the United States. The extent to which these dramatic changes will affect intermodal services in the US is difficult to predict.

We have made every effort to cover surface intermodalism as thoroughly as possible, though recognize that we may not have examined all aspects of this very broad subject in sufficient detail to satisfy everyone's interests. Nevertheless, it is our sincere wish that readers will find this book both useful and informative in their efforts to learn more about this important, fascinating transportation discipline.

DAVID R. McKENZIE
MARK C. NORTH
DANIEL S. SMITH
Oakland, California

July, 1989

PREFACE

Education is the keystone of advancement in any endeavor. That is as true in the business world as it is in academics, because a thorough command of the fundamentals of any aspect of business is crucial to one's ultimate success.

For the men and women who are participating in today's fast-changing field of international intermodal logistics, the need for education is doubly important.

This complex, new distribution science is a proving ground for new business prinicipals rooted in just-in-time inventory systems; sophisticated computer technologies; and the brave new world of transportation deregulation. Indeed, old rules are broken as new ones are made. And the new ones are subject to constant revision.

Keeping pace with, much less staying ahead of these changes is a challenging task by itself.

Fundamentals must be mastered before moving into the exciting day-to-day world of the intermodal market. For example, the meaning of the very word "intermodal" must be understood.

It has been defined by Louis A. Stock of Dow Chemical as: "Sequential use of two or more forms of transport, to complete a coordinated movement of goods." That is a good description, and is in accord with *Webster's Third New International Dictionary* which, only as recently as 1986, carried the first formal dictionary definition: "Being or involving transportation by more than one form of carrier during a single journey."

This exercise in semantics is important because the true rationale for the existence of a distinct distribution discipline known as intermodal must be clearly understood. It's purpose is not to come up with creative ways of matching modes. Rather, for any intermodal system to work it must successfully accomplish one simple task. That is, to provide the customer – the shipper – with a price and service package that is superior to anything else available.

Again, to succeed you must start by learning about the basics. What distinguishes an intermodal trailer from a standard highway trailer? TOFC/COFC, RO/RO, EDI, ANSI... what do the acronyms mean? What historical precedents have shaped current service offerings – and what impact will history have on tomorrow's intermodal networks? Who are the important players?

It is these and other fundamental questions that this useful book addresses. The authors set out to provide a basic lesson in surface-based intermodal systems and marketing, and they have succeeded.

It is my hope that by providing this necessary information for new and not-so-new members of the intermodal fraternity that we will continue the progress that has marked this young industry which has so much potential for shippers, carriers and the public at large.

Read this book... and become a better intermodalist.

Nat Welch, Chairman
International Intermodal Expo

ACKNOWLEDGEMENTS

The authors wish to acknowledge the help, support, information and encouragement given by many people during the preparation of this book.

Bill Fahrenwald, editor of *Intermodal Age International*, graciously served as our editor. Judy McCusker, of Simmons-Boardman provided valuable proofreading skills. David DeBoer, of Greenbrier Intermodal, provided both valuable insight into intermodalism and important data. John H. White, Jr., senior historian at the National Museum of American History, provided excellent background on the development of containerization on US railroads in his paper "The Magic Box: Genesis of the Container." Paul J. Capodanno, of Transamerica Container Leasing, provided feedback on the complexities of inland container and chassis logistics.

We would also like to acknowledge the following companies and organizations for providing materials and assistance:

American President Companies
Association of American Railroads
Burlington Northern
Gunderson, Inc.
Institute of International Container Lessors
International Container Leasing
Itel Rail Corporation
Manalytics, Inc.
Marathon LeTourneau
Matson Lines
Mi-Jack Products
Port of Oakland
RoadRailer®
Sea-Land, Incorporated
Smithsonian Institution
Southern Pacific Transportation Company
Steamship Operators Intermodal Committee
Taylor Machine Works
Thrall Car Manufacturing Company
Trailer Train
Transamerica Container Leasing
Trinity Industries, Inc.

V

TABLE OF CONTENTS

CHAPTER I

CHAPTER II

CHAPTER III

CHAPTER IV

CHAPTER V

CHAPTER VI

CHAPTER VII

Chapter 1

INTRODUCTION

"The intermodal revolution" is not simply the growth of new markets for the railroad industry, but a substantial change in the nation's transportation system driven by a mix of international and domestic trade requirements. Railroads, truckers, ports and steamship lines are already cooperating to develop an efficient marine-inland interface to serve this changing market. Managing their collective response to an increasingly international trade scenario will be one of the major tasks for transportation executives in the 1990s.

The railroad industry has been affected not only by rail deregulation, but by maritime and truck deregulation as well. The 1984 Shipping Act, for example, in its most general interpretation, freed ocean carriers to operate as efficiently as possible, particularly with regard to the rationalization of assets. Because steamship lines have become major buyers of railroad services, deregulation in the shipping business has had a significant impact on the railroad industry.

In terms of rail hardware developments – such as doublestack railcars and rail-highway (RoadRailer®-type) vehicles – inland transportation has changed dramatically. The long term significance of these technologies may be less than has been advertised, however, particularly in the context of the wider "revolution" transportation is experiencing in all modes. Much of that freight moves over distances too short for rail-based services ever to be competitive. But even in the over 500 mile segment, intermodal still accounts for less then 20%. Despite the contention that doublestack service will enable railroads to capture domestic traffic, in fact, analysis indicates that much of the growth of doublestack service in the domestic market is primarily the result of a shift from existing conventional COFC or TOFC services. Technological developments have not, therefore, substantially altered the respective market shares of the trucking and railroad industries. Trucking controls the majority of domestic traffic.

The growth and structure of international trade are factors that have had a far more profound effect on inland transportation than technology. In this area, the activities of the ocean carriers have thus far controlled the course of development. American President Companies' decision to build post-Panamax ships (too large to fit through the Panama Canal) for use in the trans-Pacific trade is likely to be followed in time by other major carriers. To become dependent on land-based as opposed to water-based transportation systems was a major change for an ocean carrier. The result in this shift of identity for APC from an ocean transportation service provider to a general transportation company, and now for other traditional steamship operators, has been dramatic. Increasing numbers of containers arriving at West Coast ports are destined for points inland or the East Coast. In fact, APC has apparently gained the largest market share of containerized cargo in the New York and Boston areas.

Clearly, in established corridors where the economics of doublestacking can be achieved, the railroads will provide the vital link for inland moves. Ports have recognized this and have built or are building intermodal transfer facilities specifically to handle the container movements in the marine-inland interface.

For local traffic or along corridors where double-

Figure 1-1 American President Companies stacktrains transport both international and domestic shipments between North American cities. Courtesy American President Companies.

stacking cannot be achieved economically, the trucking industry is likely to continue to control the majority of container moves. Just as the growth of the Pacific trade and the decision to build a post-Panamax vessel places an extra burden on the railroad infrastructure, so too the highway network, both urban and rural, will need to cope with increasing numbers of containers loaded with international cargos.

On the domestic front, the size of containers has become an issue. In order for ocean carriers to balance equipment moves east and west, they are becoming increasingly dependent on domestic markets for access to back-haul cargos. The economics of domestic containerization however, indicate that a nine-foot, six-inch high by 48-foot long by 102-inch wide unit is most desirable, making the common ISO 40-foot container less competitive for inland moves. Larger containers are already being used on APL and other ships in the transpacific. Use of this type of equipment in the US may affect existing highway and bridge axle-load and weight regulations.

Assuming further relaxation of Japanese regulations on larger units, the Pacific trade will experience a shift away from the ISO standard container toward a larger unit compatible with US domestic shippers' requirements, allowing ocean carriers to balance equipment requirements. A similar trend using "swap-body" units is occurring in Europe. ISO is considering broadening the scope of its dimensional criteria to include these new designs.

More significantly, the broad "industry alliances" being built through merger and acquisition by transportation firms such as CSX Corporation and Norfolk Southern are testament to the commercial reality that the transportation industry in the US can no longer be understood simply in terms of marine and inland sectors. Clearly, developments in one affect the other, increasing the burden on regulators to take a "macro" view of transportation incorporating port and terminal activities, trucking concerns, railroad issues, and ocean carrier interests.

Consequently, any government involvement needs to recognize the intertwined nature of the industry and anticipate further evolution in this direction. Effective policy making for the next decade will depend on understanding the interrelated nature of intermodal transportation and the industries involved.

Chapter 2

THE INTERMODAL PAST

The transfer of freight from one mode of transportation to another (e.g., water to rail) is certainly not a new idea. It is, in fact, a common transportation practice that has been around for thousands of years and is hardly revolutionary. However, the phenomenal growth of containerization during the past 30 years has helped to popularize the term "intermodal transportation," while simultaneously giving it a newer, stricter interpretation that centers around transferring containers (and trailers) between modes. The container certainly deserves the credit for focusing attention on intermodalism. After all, it is the container and, to a lesser extent, its wheeled cousin the piggyback trailer, that greatly simplified the age-old challenge presented by the intermodal transfer process.

Even when using the popularly accepted definition of modern intermodal transportation – the shipment of containerized cargo using more than one mode – it must be pointed out that the concept did not have its genesis in post-World War II technology, as some believe. The idea and the actual practice go back much further than that.

The Beginnings of Containerization

Perhaps the best example of an early container is the humble barrel. This forerunner of the modern shipping container has many of the same characteristics of its present day counterpart: portability, reusability and versatility. It has been used to hold many types of commodities, came in a wide range of sizes and was easily carried on ships and wagons. As testimony to its continued success through hundreds of years of service, the barrel survives today in the form of the 55-gallon drum. But when we think of the freight container now, it is usually the 20 or 40-foot (or longer) "box" hauled around on trucks, trains and ships that comes to mind, and not the barrel or drum.

Possibly the first known marriage of box-like containers to railcars occurred in England, where the Horsehay Tramway in 1792 hauled coal in iron crates to a nearby canal. At the canal the two-ton capacity crates were transferred by crane to waiting boats in what may be the original containerized, rail-water intermodal move as we now define it.

Ocean-going containers first came to America during the 1820s when Frederic Tudor began shipping ice from Boston to the tropics in chests of his own design insulated with sawdust. Because these chests were too valuable to throw away, Tudor had them returned to Massachusetts for reuse, thus creating the first empty container repositioning problem.

The fledgling American railroads also began experimenting with containers. In what is surely the precursor to modern COFC service, several of them carried wooden baggage crates on flatcars during the 1830s, 1840s and 1850s. These early containers had doors to allow for easy "stuffing" and "stripping" and wheels for moving them on and off cars.

Following the Civil War, patents for several very innovative container designs were issued. One of these was a lift-on/lift-off tank that could be transferred between wagons and flat cars. It would seem that H.J.

Lombaert, who patented this tank design in 1865, conceived the idea of the modern tank container nearly 100 years ahead of its time. Despite some clever ideas for containers, American railroads showed little interest in advancing containerization during the latter part of the 19th century.

It took another war, World War I, to revive interest in rail-borne containers. The River & Rail Transportation Co. developed a 10-foot container, the "Trinity Freight Unit," that could be carried by rail, water or road. The Freight Units came in three versions, one with side doors for general cargo, another with top and bottom doors for bulk cargo, and a third with insulation for perishables. The United States Railroad Administration, which had taken over the operation of the railroads during the war, utilized these containers.

During the same period Benjamin Franklin Fitch, working for the White Motor Co., devised a method for significantly reducing the delays caused by less-than-carload (LCL) transfers, which, at that time, were very labor and equipment intensive. Using trucks with de-mountable bodies, Fitch successfully demonstrated his LCL intermodal transfer system in Cincinnati in 1917. Not only was his method faster, it was cheaper as well. Backed by White, Fitch formed the Motor Terminals Co. to serve rail LCL traffic in the Cincinnati area, where it continued in operation until 1962.

After the war two Cincinnati interurban railroads tried out Fitch's containers, but their poor financial condition soon caused them to discontinue the service. Undaunted, Fitch developed yet another new intermodal concept, a system using flatbed trailers, flatcars, sliding transfer equipment and special insulated tanks for transporting milk from dairies to cities. The successful 1936 demonstration of his new idea led to the formation of the National Fitch Corporation in 1940. Soon thereafter many large dairies were shipping their milk using Fitch equipment. The operation lasted into the early 1950s when truck competition finally drove it out of business.

While Fitch was working hard on his intermodal ideas, others in the railroad industry were trying out containerization as well. One of the biggest names in early 20th century railroading, Alfred H. Smith, president of the New York Central, decided to experiment with containers to solve the same problem as Fitch – moving LCL shipments. Smith was deeply concerned about the high personnel and equipment costs associated with handling LCL. In the 1920s, even though LCL accounted for a mere 3% of railroad freight traffic, it accounted for nearly one-third of all damage claims. Clearly something had to be done, because as a common carrier, the Central was required to carry LCL freight and could not simply eliminate the service.

In January 1921, the New York Central made a trial run from New York to Chicago using 2,800-pound containers placed in gondola cars to carry high-value merchandise destined for department stores. Several months later the railroad signed on with the US Post Office to carry the mail in containers between New York and Chicago. Pleased with the acceptance of containers, The New York Central eventually established the LCL Corporation to promote them. Other railroads and even a major freight forwarder began to lease the steel boxes from LCL.

The Pennsylvania Railroad, not to be outdone by the Central, its chief competitor, had also started its own

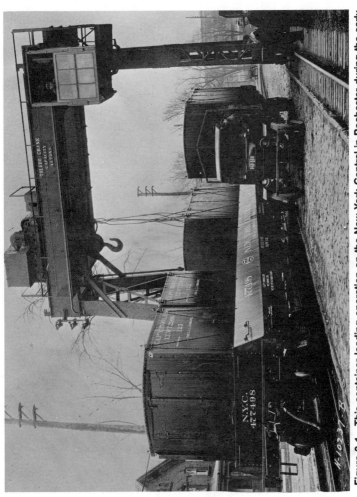

Figure 2-1 This container loading operation on the New York Central in Rochester during the early 1920s bears a strong resemblance to present-day COFC operations. Smithsonian Institution Photo No. 48,389.

container service in the late 1920s. Although their containers were very similar to the Central's, the PRR hauled them on flatcars fitted with mounting brackets rather than in gondolas. The Pennsylvania's container service was operated more like a boxcar service in that the containers were usually stuffed and stripped while still on the flatcars parked on sidings. This approach did not enable the railroad to take full advantage of the container's intermodal versatility.

Despite the efforts of Fitch, the New York Central, the Pennsylvania Railroad and others, container service on the US railroads never developed into a significant business and was all but dead by the early 1950s. Several reasons probably account for the failure of containerization to prosper, not the least of which was the lack of a major commitment on the part of the railroads themselves. It would seem that many railroaders were either unwilling to accept the new concepts or unable to because of the actions of the Interstate Commerce Commission.

Motivated by its desire to keep all modes of transportation alive and competitive with each other, the Commission apparently viewed containerization as a way of encouraging too much cooperation among the various modes. In 1931 the ICC issued a critical ruling that hindered the growth of container service and its next of kin, piggyback trailer service, for many years to come. By ruling that commodities shipped in containers must move at their carload class rates like all other types of rail shipments, rather than at flat container rates, the ICC did not allow railroads to offer cheaper rates for their container service. Without the incentive of lower rates, container service never really caught on.

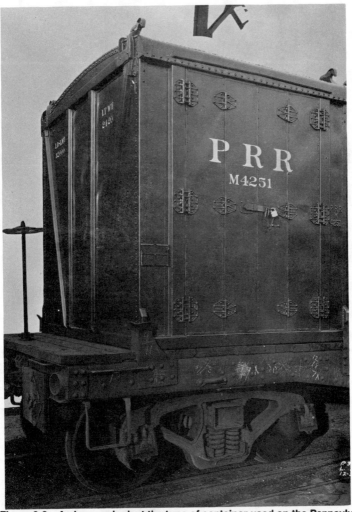

Figure 2-2   A close-up look at the type of container used on the Pennsylvania Railroad in the early 1930s. Smithsonian Institution, Pullman Collection Photo No. 36, 856

13

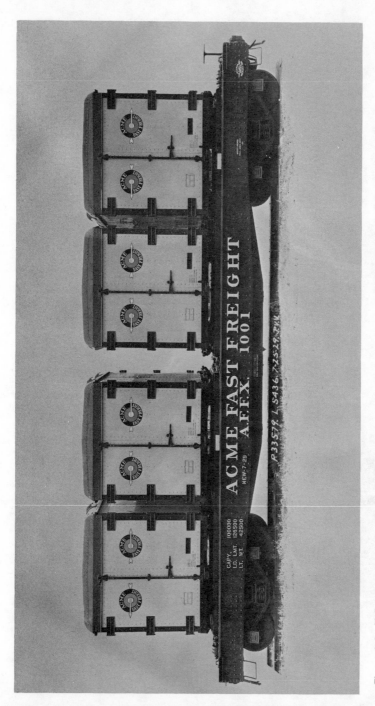

Figure 2-3 Kellet containers used by Acme Fast Freight during the 1930s. Smithsonian Institution, Pullman Collection, Photo No. 33,579.

The Container Revolution

During World War II, because military exigency demanded that cargo be moved as quickly as possible, traditional bulk methods of shipping often proved to be unacceptably slow. Traffic specialists who were pressed into military service adopted the practice of shipping mixed cargo in palletized boxes to speed up unloading at ports and distribution to the front. Taking note of these new methods, the War Shipping Administration experimented with ocean-going containers. But when the war ended interest in the new concept waned. It would be another 10 years before an innovative trucker capitalized on the wartime ideas and ushered in the "Intermodal Age."

The world's first "containership," the *Ideal-X*, made its inaugural voyage from Port Newark, N.J. on April 26, 1956. Actually it was not a true containership, but a modified T-2 tanker, and its "containers" were, in reality, 58 highway trailers. Nevertheless, this date has been named as the "birthday of the container revolution." Considering subsequent events, this appellation proved quite accurate. The man behind this momentous occasion was none other than Malcolm McLean, a trucking entrepreneur who dreamed of establishing "a coordinated land and water system for transporting freight." To implement his dream, McLean, a year earlier, had acquired the Pan Atlantic Steamship Co., which held US intercoastal shipping rights. His plans for Pan Atlantic involved using its ships as "tractors" to haul trailers in the coastwise trade. This steamship line eventually became the highly successful Sea-Land Services, with McLean as its first chairman.

McLean's container revolution very quickly moved

Figure 2-4 S.S. *Ideal-X*, the world's first "container ship" sailed on April 26, 1956. Courtesy Sea-Land Corporation.

into high gear. He soon added a second modified tanker, the *Alema,* which also had a capacity of 58 20-foot trailers. Only seven months after the *Ideal-X* sailed, Sea-Land announced plans to convert six C-2 breakbulk ships into the first cellular containerships, each with a capacity for 226 35-foot containers. The first of these entered intercoastal service between ports in New Jersey, Florida and Texas in October 1957. Because few of the ports at that time had dockside cranes suitable for containers, these first generation containerships were equipped with their own cranes.

Sea-Land did not monopolize the container revolution for long. Matson Navigation Co. kicked off the first Pacific Ocean container route when its converted C-3 freighter, the *Hawaiian Merchant,* steamed from San Francisco for Honolulu in August 1958, with 20 24-foot containers stowed on its deck. Just two years later the Grace Line initiated the first international container service between the US East Coast and ports in the Caribbean and Latin America. Not to be outdone at its own game by the competition, Sea-Land, with a fleet of containerships that had grown to 23, began the first North Atlantic container trade in 1966 by calling at ports in Germany, the Netherlands and the United Kingdom.

Today, fleets of containerships, plying all the major trade routes in the world, have virtually replaced breakbulk ships. Hundreds of steamship lines operate a combined total of over 2,100 fully or partially containerized vessels. Every major port and most smaller ones have dockside cranes designed to load and unload containers, thus eliminating the necessity for shipboard cranes.

The containerships themselves have experienced a

Figure 2-5 Matson's SS *Hawaiian Merchant* sails under the Golden Gate Bridge on August 31, 1958, inaugurating container service in the Pacific. Courtesy Matson Lines.

Figure 2-6 S.S. *Hawaiian Citizen*, formerly a World War II Navy attack transport, was converted by Matson in 1959 to a fully containerized vessel — the first in Pacific service. It had a capacity of 408 containers. Courtesy Matson Lines.

Figure 2-7 S.S. *President Adams*, a C5-class container/breakbulk ship built for American President Lines in 1968. Its capacity is 332 containers. Courtesy American President Companies.

Figure 2-8 The S.S. *Expedition*, a Sea-Land C6-class container ship. Courtesy Sea-Land Corporation.

Figure 2-9   S.S. *Matsonia*, a combination lift-on, lift-off container ship and roll-on, roll-off vehicle ship with a capacity for 500 autos. Courtesy Matson Lines.

Figure 2-10   The S.S. *Anchorage*, a D7-class container ship with a capacity of 706 containers, joined Sea-Land's Alaska trade in 1987. Courtesy Sea-Land Corporation.

remarkable evolution during the past 30 years. Since 1956 there have been four distinct generations of container carrying vessels. Figure 2-11 depicts the growth of these innovative ships from the first generation converted vessels to the fourth generation post-Panamax (i.e., too large for the Panama Canal) C-10 containerships recently commissioned by American President Lines. An even larger fifth generation (post-Panamax) vessel with an estimated length of 1,000 feet and a capacity of 4,900 20-foot equivalent units (TEUs) is predicted to appear in the mid-1990s.

As containerships began to proliferate in the 1960s so, naturally, did containers. Since no standards had been established for container dimensions, steamship lines were free to use containers sized to suit their particular requirements. For example, Sea-Land, the leader in containerization, had adopted a 35-foot box, whereas Matson was using a 24-foot box. With more and more steamship lines embracing containerization, a need for container standards was becoming clearly evident.

In 1968, the *Organisation Internationale de Normalisation* (International Standards Organization, or ISO), an international body that develops standards covering nearly all fields of technology, issued a recommendation for freight container dimensions and gross weights. Later, in 1973, this recommendation was published as ISO Standard 668 for Series 1 freight containers. It established a classification system based on external dimensions and ratings for freight containers used in intercontinental traffic. This standard has been updated twice, the last time in 1979. Other ISO Standards provide definitions and specifications for corner fittings, container testing, and lifting equipment.

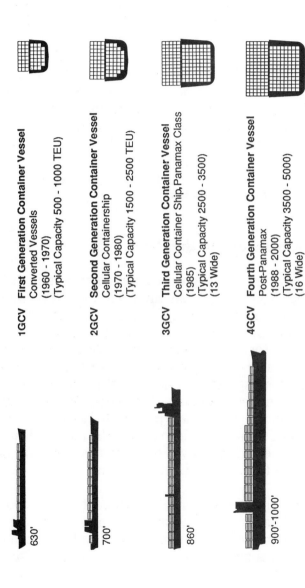

1GCV First Generation Container Vessel
Converted Vessels
(1960 - 1970)
(Typical Capacity 500 - 1000 TEU)

630'

2GCV Second Generation Container Vessel
Cellular Containership
(1970 - 1980)
(Typical Capacity 1500 - 2500 TEU)

700'

3GCV Third Generation Container Vessel
Cellular Container Ship,Panamax Class
(1985)
(Typical Capacity 2500 - 3500)
(13 Wide)

860'

4GCV Fourth Generation Container Vessel
Post-Panamax
(1988 - 2000)
(Typical Capacity 3500 - 5000)
(16 Wide)

900'-1000'

Figure 2-11   © Vickerman Zachary Miller 1988

25

Like the containership, the container, too, has evolved since the beginning of the revolution. They now come in many lengths, ranging from 10 to 45 feet for marine containers and the longer 48- and 53-foot lengths for "domestic" containers. Container heights also vary, from the standard 8 feet to the "high-cube" 9 feet 6 inches. Many different types have been developed to meet a variety of shipping needs. Besides the general purpose dry box container there are many special purpose types, including insulated, refrigerated, open top, platform (without side walls), tank (tanks within a framework), and dry bulk (similar to tank containers). Altogether, the worldwide container population is estimated at nearly five million.

Containers Return to the Rails

The door was reopened for rail containers in 1954, when the ICC, in a case involving the New Haven Railroad, ruled that hauling trailers on flatcars was, indeed, transportation by rail and, therefore, did not require a motor-carrier certificate. Although this ruling was for a trailer-on-flatcar (TOFC) case it did have the effect of reversing the 1931 decision that had so severely impacted container service. That decision encouraged the railroads to expand their previously lackluster TOFC service, and, along with the arrival of the modern marine container, helped to pave the way for present day container-on-flatcar (COFC) rail service.

During the 1960s, marine containers began to appear on the railroads; however, rail intermodal traffic during that time remained predominantly TOFC. In a prophecy of things to come, one railroad, the Southern Pacific, reported in the December 1967, issue of its company magazine, "While the highway trailer is still the principle container for piggyback, SP is developing new container services, particularly in cooperation with steamship lines."

The SP magazine was portending the development of "landbridge" service. Landbridge is an intermodal movement in which containers are transferred from a ship to a train at a port on one coast, then transported across the country to a port on the other coast and transferred back to another ship. The goods pass through the US from an overseas origin to an overseas destination, e.g., the Far East and Europe. Landbridge, which saves significant time over an all-water move through the Panama Canal, was formally introduced to the US in 1972 by Sea-Land.

Two variations of landbridge include "minibridge" and "microbridge." Minibridge, which was introduced by SeaTrain in 1972, is an intermodal movement where the container traffic terminates at the second port, e.g., from the Far East through Los Angeles, then via rail to its destination at New York. Like landbridge, this move saves time over an all-water move. The microbridge connects ocean container traffic with an inland origin or destination.

The 1970s saw a steady growth in landbridge traffic as more containerships entered service and world trade patterns began to shift. Europe's role as the dominant overseas trading partner of the US was declining with the steady rise in competitively priced exports from the emerging Pacific Rim countries. To be sure, many of the Far Eastern goods entering West Coast ports had destinations on the West Coast; but many more were bound for the large population centers in the Midwest and the East, and even for Europe. Needless to say, the influx of these goods gave a big boost to landbridge moves.

Late in the 1970s, in an effort to gain better control of the inland movement of its cargo, American President Lines negotiated with the railroads (UP & CNW) for its own dedicated trains, thus introducing the "Linertrain" concept in 1979. These APL Linertrains ran on set schedules coordinated with ship movements. With its own leased flatcars, APL was assured of having an adequate amount of equipment available when needed, particularly when the railroads were experiencing car shortages.

Perhaps the biggest technological breakthrough for rail container service was the doublestack container car, the first railcar designed from the wheels up exclusively to carry containers. Earlier rail containers had been carried either on flatcars or in gondola cars. When marine containers began to ride the rails they had to share space with trailers on piggyback flatcars. But with the appearance of the doublestack car, a much more efficient means of hauling containers by rail became available.

Southern Pacific was the first railroad to develop and test the doublestack concept. As early as 1971 SP engineers began work on a doublestack car design. Working with ACF Industries, Southern Pacific built the first doublestack – a bulkhead-type car – in 1977. Used in regular operation, this prototype hauled two 40-foot containers between West and Gulf Coast terminals, successfully demonstrating its capability. Pleased with the results, SP procured several three-unit articulated doublestack prototypes in 1979 for additional testing. In 1981, the railroad bought 42 five-unit articulated double-stack cars from ACF and placed them into service between Los Angeles and Houston.

Evidently American President Lines was watching the doublestack developments closely. Having already entered the "railroad business" through its Linertrain operation, APL decided to test its own doublestack cars in 1983. Convinced it was a promising concept, APL, early in 1984, took the bold step of offering regularly scheduled doublestack unit train service. Other steamship lines and all the major US railroads soon followed APL's lead by establishing their own doublestack train service. Numerous high-priority doublestack trains now crisscross the nation every day.

The doublestack car APL selected for its service differed in design from the original bulkhead car SP developed. Instead of utilizing bulkheads to secure the upper container in place, the APL car uses interbox connectors (IBCs) similar to those used on containerships for securing containers. Although the interbox connector car has five articulated platforms capable of carrying ten 40-foot containers like the bulkhead car, it has less tare weight.

Doublestack cars of both types have dramatically improved the efficiency with which railroads can haul containers. A 20-car doublestack train, which is approximately one mile long, can carry 200 40-foot containers. The equivalent length COFC train can only carry about 110 40-foot containers. Doublestack trains, because of the cars' lighter tare weight and improved aerodynamics, offer an estimated 40% fuel savings over conventional trains. Furthermore, since their cars are articulated, doublestack trains have only one-fifth the number of couplers, thus substantially reducing the slack action. Slack action, which occurs whenever a train stretches or

Figure 2-12   APL IBC-type double-stack car. Courtesy Thrall Car Manufacturing Company.

30

contracts, can cause damage to lading if it is severe enough.

Although it may not necessarily have been planned, doublestack cars have helped to foster the use of marine containers in domestic service. Because the predominant flow of international container traffic moves through the US from west to east there is a need to reposition containers back to the West Coast as quickly as possible. Faced with the possibility of moving empty containers, steamship lines were in a position to sell space at very competitive rates to domestic (and international) shippers sending goods westbound. The success of using marine containers for domestic traffic encouraged the introduction of the "pure" domestic 48- and 53-foot containers. Thus, doublestack cars helped to usher in the age of domestic containerization.

The History of Piggyback Trailer Service

Although much of the current attention given to intermodalism has centered around containers, the contribution of piggyback trailers to the development of intermodal transportation cannot be minimized. Until the mid-1980s boom in doublestack container trains, "pigs," as trailers on flatcars are commonly known, were the dominant form of inland intermodal service.

The piggyback concept of placing wagons and carriages on flatcars goes back to the beginnings of railroading in the 1830s. One of the most colorful early uses of piggyback began in 1872 when P. T. Barnum's circus used end ramps to load and unload circus wagons on and off flatcars. This method gave rise to the term "circus loading," a common TOFC loading practice replaced by

31

mechanized lift equipment in the 70's.

The prototype for modern piggyback trailer service began over 60 years ago on the Chicago, North Shore and Milwaukee Railroad in 1926. In its "ferry truck" service, the North Shore used its own 16-foot trailers and specially built flatcars to carry merchandise traffic between Chicago and Milwaukee in a move to counter growing motor carrier competition. The North Shore's service was similar to present-day Plan II piggybacking (Figure 2-13) in that the railroad offered door-to-door pickup and delivery of LCL freight in trailers that required no transfer of lading enroute. Rates were published on a flat, all-merchandise basis, subject to a minimum weight requirement.

During the latter part of the 1930s, The Chicago Great Western Railway Company and the New York, New Haven and Hartford Railroad both experimented with ramp-to-ramp piggyback services similar to TOFC Plans I and III. Concerned about the growth of independent trucking companies not subject to route or rate regulation and therefore capable of providing very flexible pickup and delivery service, these railroads were attempting to encourage the truckers to ship their trailers by rail rather than haul them over the highways. These efforts, however, generated very little TOFC traffic.

As with COFC service, TOFC service languished during the 1940s and early 1950s. But the New Haven decision of 1954 proved to be a major breakthrough for TOFC service and helped to turn the corner on TOFC traffic growth. Just a few years later, in 1957, the AAR reported that its member railroads hauled 249,065 TOFC/COFC carloads. As early AAR data did not distinguish between trailers and containers, it is not

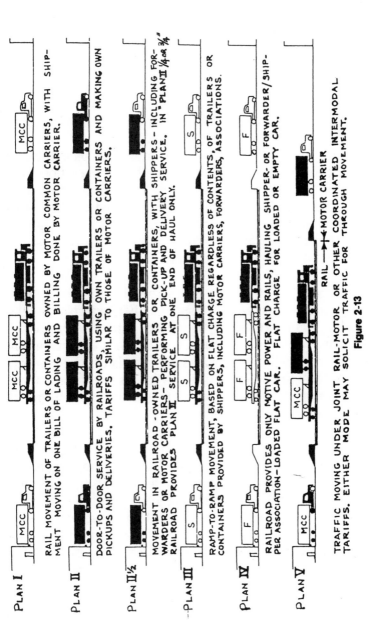

PLAN I

RAIL MOVEMENT OF TRAILERS OR CONTAINERS OWNED BY MOTOR COMMON CARRIERS, WITH SHIPMENT MOVING ON ONE BILL OF LADING AND BILLING DONE BY MOTOR CARRIER.

PLAN II

DOOR-TO-DOOR SERVICE BY RAILROADS, USING OWN TRAILERS OR CONTAINERS AND MAKING OWN PICKUPS AND DELIVERIES, TARIFFS SIMILAR TO THOSE OF MOTOR CARRIERS.

PLAN II½

MOVEMENT IN RAILROAD-OWNED TRAILERS OR CONTAINERS, WITH SHIPPERS - INCLUDING FORWARDERS OR MOTOR CARRIERS - PERFORMING PICK-UP AND DELIVERY SERVICE. IN "PLAN II ¼ OR ¾" RAILROAD PROVIDES PLAN II SERVICE AT ONE END OF HAUL ONLY.

PLAN III

RAMP-TO-RAMP MOVEMENT, BASED ON FLAT CHARGE REGARDLESS OF CONTENTS, OF TRAILERS OR CONTAINERS PROVIDED BY SHIPPERS, INCLUDING MOTOR CARRIERS, FORWARDERS, ASSOCIATIONS.

PLAN IV

RAILROAD PROVIDES ONLY MOTIVE POWER AND RAILS, HAULING SHIPPER- OR FORWARDER/SHIPPER ASSOCIATION-LOADED FLAT CAR. FLAT CHARGE FOR LOADED OR EMPTY CAR.

PLAN V

TRAFFIC MOVING UNDER JOINT RAIL-MOTOR OR OTHER COORDINATED INTERMODAL TARIFFS. EITHER MODE MAY SOLICIT TRAFFIC FOR THROUGH MOVEMENT.

RAIL ——————►◄—— MOTOR CARRIER

Figure 2-13

33

possible to determine the precise ratio of trailers to containers. However, since marine containers were relatively new on the scene at that time, the vast majority of these loadings probably involved trailers.

Recognizing the increasing importance of TOFC traffic to their operations, the Pennsylvania Railroad and the Norfolk and Western Railway met in November 1955, to incorporate the Trailer Train Company, a car pooling venture intended to foster the growth of piggybacking. The following March, Trailer Train began operations with a fleet of 500 used 75-foot flatcars, each capable of carrying two 35-foot trailers. By the end of 1988 stock ownership in the company had increased to 19 railroads and the intermodal fleet size had grown to over 44,000 cars (or over 96,000 intermodal platforms).

Trailer Train has been at the forefront of modern piggyback equipment development. For example, in 1958 Trailer Train introduced the trailer hitch as a means of securing a trailer to a flatcar's deck, thus eliminating the need for winches and chains. A year later, the company placed the first 85-foot flatcars in service to accommodate two of the newer 40-foot trailers that were beginning to replace the older 35-footers.

As trailers continued to grow in length, Trailer Train met the challenge. In 1980 the company implemented a program to modify the hitch arrangement on its 89-foot piggyback flatcars (the longest cars permitted on most US railroads) so that two 45-foot trailers, which were now replacing the 40-footers, could be carried. With the passage of the Surface Transportation Assistance Act of 1982 48-foot long (and 102-inch wide) trailers were permitted to operate on designated highways throughout the nation without state interference. Since it was not

Figure 2-14 75-foot "TTX" Trailer Train flat car loaded with two 35-foot trailers. Courtesy Trailer Train Company.

35

physically possible to carry two 48-footers on an 89-foot flatcar, Trailer Train went back to the drawing boards and, in 1983, introduced the "Front Runner," a 50-foot, low-level, flatcar equipped with single-axle trucks and capable of carrying a single trailer from 40 to 48 feet in length and up to 102 inches in width. Faced with yet an even longer 53-foot trailer, the company, in 1987, brought out its "Long Runner," two 89-foot flatcars permanently connected by a drawbar. This behemoth is capable of carrying three 53-foot trailers or even three 57-foot trailers (if and when they are ever built).

Interest in developing new TOFC car designs was not limited to Trailer Train alone. Larry Cena of the Santa Fe pioneered the six-pack in 1975. In 1978, the Santa Fe Railway introduced the "Ten-Pack Fuel Foiler," a skeletonized railcar with 10 articulated platforms each capable of carrying a trailer. Santa Fe even experimented with specially designed "A-Stack" containers which could be loaded onto the Fuel-Foilers by straddling the cars' center beams. The ITEL Corporation acquired the rights to the Fuel Foilers, made some changes to the design, and marketed under the name "Impack" a car in 4-, 5-, 8-, and 10-platform versions. American Car & Foundry, in 1981, came out with "4 – Runner," a single-axle, articulated car with four platforms each capable of handling a single 45-foot trailer.

During the 1970s and early 1980s the demand for more TOFC cars to accommodate the expanding piggy-back market encouraged several railroads and car-leasing companies to embark on programs to convert other types of rolling stock to TOFC use. The superstructures were removed from boxcars to convert them into flatcars capable of carrying single trailers. Bulkhead flatcars had their bulkheads removed and hitches added. Even conven-

Figure 2-15   Ten-platform version of Itels "Impack" trailer car. Courtesy Itel Rail Corporation

tional flatcars had hitches added to make them suitable for TOFC use.

The future of TOFC service is the source of considerable debate in the freight transportation industry. Some industry pundits believe that piggyback trailers will soon become a thing of the past, as newer, better technologies take over. Others view TOFC with optimism, believing that there will always be a place for piggyback trailers on some corridors. Despite the fact that the piggyback trailer fleet is aging, the pig is not yet dead. These older trailers, which are 40 and 45 feet long, and 96 inches wide, are gradually being replaced by the construction of new 45- and 48-foot long, 102-inch wide, "high-cube" piggyback trailers. Even though the building of new pigs continues, the advent of doublestack trains and the rise of domestic containerization has caused many carriers and shippers to closely examine the benefits of TOFC.

"Carless" Technology

Engineers who design transportation equipment have long sought to maximize their vehicles' net-to-tare ratios (i.e., the ratio of the weight of the goods to the weight of the vehicle). The reasons are quite simple: the higher the net-to-tare ratio, the lower the fuel costs per revenue ton-mile. And, reduced tare weight permits increased freight-carrying capacity within legal limits. Because trailers on flatcars have lower net-to-tare ratios than boxcars, some of TOFC's service benefits are offset by TOFC's higher fuel costs per revenue ton-mile.

Equipment designers realized that if a way could be found to eliminate the railcar part of the intermodal system altogether, the overall tare weight (i.e., the sum of the trailer or container and flatcar weights) could be greatly reduced and, consequently, the net-to-tare ratio greatly increased. The Chesapeake & Ohio Railroad came up with a way to do exactly that in 1959 when it introduced "Rail Van" service. The C&O took 80 26-foot single axle trailers (later nicknamed "pups" because of their short length) and added single-axle rail wheels and special hitches to them. A mechanical mechanism was used to retract the rubber-tired highway wheels out of the way during rail operations.

Because the Rail Van trailers lacked the standard safety appliances required for freight cars, the C&O had to operate them coupled to the ends of passenger trains. This arrangement provided the lading a much better ride than it would have experienced on freight trains because there was considerably less slack action on the passenger trains. The C&O offered the service, which carried primarily mail and small packages, between Chicago and Michigan for 10 years until 1969 when the railroad discontinued passenger service.

The Rail Van, or "RoadRailer®" as C&O called it, may well have died a natural death if it were not for Robert Reebie, a former vice president of strategic planning for the New York Central, who picked up the concept. Reebie, who had concluded that the economics of TOFC could not compete against highway service in the short-haul market, bought the rights to the Road-Railer® name from the Chessie. Convinced that the technology would work, he formed the Bi-Modal Corporation, which ultimately produced two prototype 45-foot by 96-inch "Mark IV" RoadRailers® in 1978. These two rail-highway trailers were successfully tested at the Transportation Test Center in Pueblo, Colo.

In 1980, Tiger International, parent company of Flying Tiger, bought Bi-Modal and placed it under its North American Car Corporation. That same year 250 RoadRailers® were built and tested on the Seaboard System. Eventually, RoadRailers® were tested on the Illinois Central Gulf, Burlington Northern, and Conrail. Several years later, because of bankruptcy proceedings involving North American Car, the RoadRailer® program stagnated. However, late in 1985, Duchossois Industries, owner of Thrall Car Manufacturing Company (a maker of doublestack cars) bought RoadRailer® and things began to improve for the company.

With the purchase of 750 RoadRailers® in 1987 by Norfolk Southern, business picked up dramatically for RoadRailer®. The Norfolk Southern placed the bi-modal trailers into its Triple Crown program, a dedicated unit-train service operating from a hub in Fort Wayne, Ind., to Chicago, St. Louis, Detroit and Atlanta. NS subsequently acquired another 250 Mark IVs and 600 of the newer Mark Vs with detachable rail bogies, increasing its fleet of RoadRailers® to 1,600. CSX Logistics has also accepted delivery of 250 of the larger Mark IV units for its "XpressRailer" service between Detroit and Atlanta. Mark Vs were briefly used on the Union Pacific in 1988 between Chicago and Dallas. By early 1989 over 2000 RoadRailers® of both types had been built.

Other companies have also explored the carless technology concept. One of these, Railmaster System, Inc., conceived the idea of combining a modified Fruehauf "Z" van with a detachable standard 70-ton rail truck. Railmaster was eventually absorbed by RoadRailer® and its idea appeared as the Mark V Roadrailer®. Fastrack Freightways has also been developing a Mark V-type

Figure 2-16   Early Mark IV RoadRailer in highway mode. Courtesy RoadRailer.

Figure 2-17   Mark V RoadRailers undergoing testing at the Transportation Test Center in Pueblo, Colo. Courtesy RoadRailer.

trailer with an air suspension system. The latest contender in this market is the Strick Corporation, which in partnership with Sambre et Meuse of France has developed the RailTrailer, a system in which two highway vans share a detachable bogie. The vans are attached to the bogie by means of an aperture/twistlock connection. Prototype testing of the RailTrailers has been completed.

The RoadRailer® is the only example of the carless technology that has been placed into revenue service, giving the RoadRailer® Company an early advantage in the marketplace. With the exception of the Mark IV and Mark V RoadRailers®, none of these carless technology designs is compatible with another. As a consequence, a carrier selecting a design has compelling reasons to stay with that particular design to the exclusion of others.

Deregulation

The need for regulatory reform of the railroad industry became increasingly evident as the industry's financial woes became more and more serious during the 1950s and 1960s. Even though many of these problems were, in fact, due to growing competition from the burgeoning motor carrier industry and to other non-regulatory factors, economic regulation was proving to be a major contributor to the industry's decline. Not only did the railroad industry as a whole stand to gain from deregulation, but specialized rail services, such as intermodal, would benefit greatly as well.

Proponents of regulatory reform offered the following arguments in favor of deregulation:

– The economic regulation in place had failed to

provide a sound railroad system that served the public well.

– Regulation was too restrictive and hampered management's ability to solve problems, particularly in dealing with such issues as rate-making, mergers and line abandonments.

– Market forces could do a much better job than government regulation in determining what services should be provided and at what rates.

The movement to liberalize the economic regulation of railroads was given a tremendous boost by the bankruptcy of the Penn Central in 1970, just two years after the new railroad was created from the ailing New York Central and the Pennsylvania Railroad. In 1973 Congress passed the Regional Rail Reorganization (3R) Act that created the United States Railroad Association, a non-profit planning organization given the mandate to restructure the northeastern railroad network. The 3R Act also created Conrail, a for-profit company intended to operate the restructured rail system. Although the 3R Act did not deal with economic reform issues *per se*, it did provide positive signs that Congress was at long last concerned enough about saving the railroad industry to take some action.

Railroad regulatory reform bills supported by the Department of Transportation were introduced to Congress in 1971 and 1974, but neither passed. Finally, in 1976, Congress passed the Railroad Revitalization and Regulatory Reform (4R) Act. The 4R Act (besides providing funding for Conrail) allowed the ICC to exempt certain traffic under certain circumstances. The Act, by providing for some relaxation of the regulation of railroad rates and changes in the regulation of mergers and line abandonments, paved the way for more serious regulatory reform.

Another step down the road to deregulation occurred in 1978 when the ICC, under Ex Parte 358-F, permitted railroads to enter into contract rate agreements with their customers, a practice which previously was prohibited because it was viewed as anti-competitive and discriminatory. The railroads' ability to make contracts with their shippers proved to be a very important element in the success of the innovative intermodal services developed during the 1980s.

Certainly the greatest boon to railroad deregulation came with the passage of the Staggers Act of 1980, which amended the Interstate Commerce Act. This momentous piece of legislation lifted much of the regulatory burden that had encumbered railroads since the passage of the original Interstate Commerce Act in 1887. Whereas the 4R Act provided for "relaxation" in the regulation of rail rates, mergers and abandonments, the Staggers Act provided for substantial reform in regulating these areas. In particular, the Staggers Act gave the railroads a considerable amount of latitude in determining and modifying rates without the ICC's interference. The AAR has noted that under Staggers as many as two-thirds of all railroad rates were no longer affected by maximum rate regulation requirements. The Staggers Act also backed up the earlier ICC ruling on contracts by permitting contract carriage by rail common carriers.

Using its authority granted under the 4R and Staggers Acts, the ICC, in 1981, exempted from rate regulation all rail and truck service provided in railroad equipment in conjunction with TOFC and COFC service. This exemption, which applied to both rail/truck and rail/ocean carrier intermodal operations, made it far easier for railroads to compete against truck and barge operators. Naturally, the motor carrier industry was not pleased with the ICC ruling and fought unsuccessfully to have it overturned. In 1984 the ICC eliminated all remaining TOFC/COFC traffic rate regulation when it ruled that even TOFC/COFC freight carried by independent (i.e., non-railroad owned) motor carriers was exempted, if at least part of the movement was by rail.

As the result of another significant piece of transportation legislation, the Motor Carrier Act of 1980, a motor carrier was allowed to interchange a TOFC trailer with a railroad at any point, as long as origin and destination points were within the motor carrier's operating permit, even when the point of interchange was not.

Not only has deregulation breathed new life into the railroads, it has greatly enhanced the development of intermodal services. The freedom to set and change rates without needing permission from the ICC, a cumbersome and time-consuming process at best, places railroad intermodal services in a much better position to compete more effectively against other modes, particularly long-haul trucking. Furthermore, the ability to make contracts helps to maximize the benefits of new intermodal technology, as in the case of American President Lines' 10-year agreement with the Union Pacific Railroad to haul the steamship line's doublestack trains.

Container and trailer volume statistics clearly confirm the improvements brought about by deregulation. From 1980 (the last year of regulation) to 1981, container/trailer loadings increased by 3%, from 3.1 million to 3.2

million. What is so remarkable about this gain is that it occurred for the first time in a recession year. In 1982, volume increased to 3.4 million, a 6% increase, despite the continuing recession. The following year volume jumped to 4.1 million, a whopping 21% increase from 1982. The upward trend has continued ever since, although percentage growth was not as spectacular in the late 1980s.

The Emergence of Multi-Modal Transportation Companies

Even giving due consideration to the new technologies, one of the most exciting developments of the intermodal revolution has been the creation of companies that provide door-to-door transportation services through fully integrated intermodal networks. These "multimodal" (or "total") transportation companies have assembled the management expertise to coordinate complex international movements of containerized cargo through a system that links together all three surface transportation modes – ocean, rail and highway. To be sure, much of the success of these companies can be attributed to dramatic improvements in both transportation equipment and electronic information handling technology, as well as to having the freedom to operate in a substantially deregulated environment. But it took people with skill, vision and daring to put all the diverse components together and make them work reliably and efficiently.

American President Lines was one of the first transportation companies to make the commitment to becoming a truly intermodal transportation company. Although APL, the forerunner of American President Companies (APC), may not have been the first steamship line to fully embrace containerization, it was certainly at the forefront of those that recognized the need for establishing an inland transportation network under its own control.

APL laid the groundwork in the 1970s for its present day intermodal operations while it was still part of Natomas Company. Under the leadership of Bruce Seaton, who became president and chief executive officer of APL in 1976, the steamship line began to forge a tightly linked intermodal transportation chain that connected the Indian Ocean and Pacific Rim to the East Coast of North America. In the winter of 1977, APL faced a transportation crisis of major proportions. Blizzards and strikes had left much of the highway network in the eastern two-thirds of the US virtually immobilized. Thus, leaving the movement of thousands of APL's containers on the East Coast to be controlled by the railroads, which, at that point in time, were unable to properly track.

The electronic data system that APL had painstakingly developed to track equipment, route cargo, store bill of lading information and perform other vital traffic functions previously done manually only covered the ocean portion of cargo movements. Once the containers were off-loaded from the ships at West Coast ports and placed on trucks or railcars for the inland portion of the move, APL had no capability to track them or exercise any control over them. Furthermore, the domestic carriers often had difficulties understanding the ocean carrier's documentation. So a system that worked only marginally well under the best of circumstances nearly collapsed when bad weather and other service disruptions occurred.

Faced with no other choice, APL decided to take its destiny into its own hands. First, Seaton assembled a team of experts to handle the immediate problem of finding APL's containers and getting them moving again. With that taken care of, APL embarked on a plan to prevent similar problems from happening again.

APL began to recruit managers with expertise in domestic transportation to form an operations team that could turn APL into an intermodal company. One of its first endeavors was to develop a program to contract for dedicated trains to carry APL's containers, thus giving birth to the Linertrain concept in 1979. To ensure against car shortages, a common problem in the past, APL started leasing its own railcars. Eventually, the steamship line also acquired its own intermodal terminals. The computerized container tracking system was expanded to cover domestic movements throughout the US.

The next step for APL, now that it had virtually become an inland carrier, was to find a way to maximize the use of its equipment. Since most of the steamship line's traffic was imported goods destined for the population centers in the eastern third of the US, its containers were returned to the West Coast empty once the goods were delivered. This was hardly the way to achieve maximum utilization of millions of dollars worth of boxes, not to mention having the added burden of paying to move empties. APL reached an agreement with Transway International, a surface freight forwarder, in which Transway solicited cargo for APL's containers returning to the West Coast. Through this arrangement, APL was able to achieve much improved utilization of its equipment.

In 1983, as part of the merger agreement between

the Natomas Company and the Diamond Shamrock Corporation, APL became part of a publicly traded corporation known as American President Companies. That same year APC successfully tested its first doublestack Linertrains, which were put into regularly scheduled service the following year. Having demonstrated to itself the very positive benefits of working with a freight forwarder (Transway) to secure backhaul traffic, APC acquired its own shipper's agent, National Piggyback Services, and an auto parts distribution service, Intermodal Brokerage Services, both from the Brae Corporation in 1985. American President Intermodal (API) was also formed in 1985 to operate the doublestack train network.

APC's "total transportation" company structure continued to evolve into its present-day organization. Early in 1987 American President Domestic (APD) was established as a peer to APL to provide overall management of domestic transportation services. National Piggyback, renamed American President Distribution Services (APDS), Intermodal Brokerage Services, renamed American President Automotive Distribution (APAD), and API were all placed under APD. In 1988 American President Trucking, a drayage and long haul support trucking company, was formed and also placed under APD. Today, APC provides the complete intermodal transportation package – the ships, the railcars, the trucks, and the management services that tie them all together.

CSX/Sea-Land Intermodal (CSL Intermodal) came into being in quite a different way than APC. The CSX portion of the name is the result of a merger between the Cleveland-based Chessie System railroad and the Jacksonville-based (Seaboard System railroad) late in 1980. The Sea-Land portion is, of course, none other than Sea-Land Service, the containership line formed by Malcolm

McLean, the "father of containerization," in 1956. Through its acquisition of Sea-Land in 1987 CSX became the first US transportation company to own both a major railroad and a major steamship line. In fact, the ICC had to approve the acquisition under provisions of the Panama Canal Act of 1912, which governs mergers between rail and ocean carriers.

Being the prototype containership line, inaugurating the first container service in 1956, Sea-Land brought with it an extensive intermodal background. In 1972 Sea-Land introduced the landbridge concept to the US. The steamship line also began a program that offered inland cargo delivery on a single through bill of lading. It was actually Sea-Land that tested the first doublestack cars in a joint project with Southern Pacific in 1980, but it was not until 1985 that the steamship line purchased double-stack cars and commenced regularly scheduled unit train service between Tacoma, Wash., and Little Ferry, N.J.

Prior to acquiring Sea-Land, the CSX Corporation had split the railroad up into three quasi-autonomous functional groups under CSX Transportation: CSX Distribution Services to handle marketing, CSX Rail Transport for operations and CSX Equipment. Once Sea-Land came aboard, CSX was faced with the challenge of how to integrate the railroad intermodal operations with those of the containership line. Almost immediately, CSX initiated a program to establish a separate intermodal operations unit. Under this program, all of CSX Distribution Services' intermodal activities (which were an amalgamation of Chessie's and Seaboard's intermodal operations) and Sea-Land's inland intermodal services group were brought together in January 1988. The result was CSL Intermodal, a new and distinct group, with M. McNeil Porter, former Sea-Land vice president-Asia, as its president.

Figure 2-18 The first production version of Gunderson's "Twin-Stack" bulkhead double-stack car carrying sea-land containers. Courtesy Gunderson, Inc.

Also placed under CSL Intermodal was CMX Trucking, the Chessie's former trucking subsidiary. CMX Trucking provides drayage services at a number of CSL Intermodal's terminals.

Comparisons to the organization of American President Companies' intermodal operations are inevitable. For example, CSL Intermodal can be classified as a "non-railroad-owning train operator," much like American President Intermodal, APC's doublestack operating arm. As with API, CSL Intermodal's mandate is to sign up as much traffic as possible for its high capacity doublestack train service. However, there is a difference: CSL Intermodal has access to an in-house railroad that covers much of the eastern US, a benefit API does not have. On the other hand, API does have access to APDS, its own in-house "third party," to retail its doublestack services; CSL Intermodal, primarily wholesales to outside third parties, who, in turn perform, the retail services, an important distinction between the two total transportation companies. Differences aside, CSL Intermodal, like APC, can provide its customers all three modes – sea, rail and highway – linked together with comprehensive electronic data interchange services.

In sharp contrast to the capital intensive approach to total transportation services adopted by both APC and CSL Intermodal, Burlington Northern Worldwide, a wholly-owned subsidiary of the BN Railroad, made a strategic decision not to own any equipment assets. Opened for business in January 1988, the same month as CSL Intermodal, BN Worldwide offers its customers worldwide door-to-door service using a single bill of lading, without operating any vehicles. Through leases, slot charters, and various contractual arrangements with several carriers, BN Worldwide can offer the same frequency of service as any large equipment-operating transportation company.

BN Worldwide has established a network of participants under its wing, including: customs brokers, freight forwarders, overseas agents, consolidators, truckers, railroads, steamship lines and non-vessel operating common carriers (NVOCCs). Difficult to classify because of its unique nature, the company has been described as a broker by some industry analysts. However, BN Worldwide seems to prefer thinking of itself as a "super NVOCC." Perhaps the "super" appellation is justified, considering the expansive range of services offered:

– LTL/LCL/FCL shipments

– Chartering of ocean vessels for transporting full, partial, and project cargos

– International air freight

– Consolidation/distribution/warehousing

– Logistics management

Despite being owned by a railroad, BN Worldwide is operated at arms length from its parent and has complete freedom to use any US railroad it feels offers the customer the best price, service and routing.

Not all the transportation companies offering integrated inland intermodal services in the US are American owned. Foreign-flag steamship lines were quick to follow their US counterparts in establishing doublestack train programs. The Rail-Bridge Corporation was set up as a

54

wholly-owned US subsidiary of "K" Line (Kawaski Kisen Kaisha, Ltd.) to operate the Japanese ocean carrier's doublestack service. Two other Japanese lines, Mitsui O.S.K. Lines (MOL) and Nippon Yusen Kaisha (NYK) line, as well as the Danish line Maersk, the Hong Kong line Orient Overseas Container Line (OOCL), Singapore's Neptune Orient Lines (NOL), and Evergreen Line of Taiwan also schedule doublestack trains and provide related intermodal services.

Growth of Rail Intermodal Traffic

Intermodal traffic on the railroads began to increase steadily from the mid-1950s to 1980 as depicted in Figure 2-19. Probably two of the main factors that provided the impetus for growth in this period were the favorable ICC decision in the New Haven case and the appearance of marine containers in ever larger numbers. By 1980 the AAR was reporting over 1.6 million intermodal carloadings (3.1 million trailers and containers) after reaching a peak in 1979 of nearly 1.9 carloadings (3.3 million trailers and containers). The tremendous growth of containerized freight between the mid-50s and 1980 would strongly suggest that a growing portion of these carloadings late in this time period included containers.

The 1980s have seen an even more dramatic increase in railroad intermodal traffic. In 1988, over 5.7 million trailers and containers were carried by American railroads, an 87% increase from the nearly 3.1 million carried in 1980. Conrail set a record in 1987 as the first railroad to transport over one million intermodal units in a single year, and repeated that accomplishment in 1988. Intermodal carloadings have now achieved second place behind coal in rank of carloadings by commodity group.

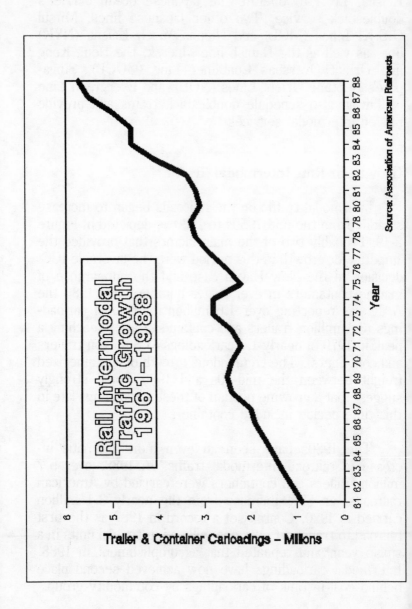

Rail Intermodal
Traffic Growth
1961-1988

Traller & Container Carloadings – Millions

Year

Source: Association of American Railroads

Much of the growth in intermodal traffic between 1980 and 1988 can probably be attributed to the greater freedom from regulatory restraints granted under the Staggers Act, fundamental changes in the US economy and trade patterns, and new technological developments, the most notable being doublestack cars. With railroads, steamship lines, and third parties aggressively marketing intermodal services, this growth should continue, as long as no reversals occur in the regulatory arena and as long as the US economy remains strong.

Chapter 3

INTERMODAL EQUIPMENT

One of the major factors affecting the efficiency of a transportation system is the availability of the hardware required to make an idea work. This is particularly true when we look at intermodal transportation, where the idea of using a combination of railroad cars, ships, trucks and barges to carry goods from point to point depends on the existence and ready availability of suitable equipment – containers, specialized railcars, cellular vessels, chassis, cranes, etc. Intermodalism, precisely because it involves moving from one mode to another, has some very specific hardware requirements, perhaps more so than any other system for moving general cargo.

To take advantages of intermodalism, carriers rely heavily on technology. Not surprisingly, therefore, the "intermodal revolution" has been understood not only as a marketing phenomenon, but also as a technological one. Engineers and designers are not simply providing the technological answers to logistic problems, but are actually creating logistic possibilities. "We can now do what we've always wanted to do," as one industry executive put it.

The extent to which technology has responded to the modern intermodal market has been substantial. Initially the development was fueled by tremendous volumes of international cargo originating in the Pacific Basin and moving eastbound across continental North America. Now, however, technological development is responding much more to the needs of the domestic intermodal market. The newest intermodal rail technology features railcars designed and built exclusively to carry containers (both domestic and ISO sizes), modifications of existing hardware to meet intermodal market demand and the continuing emergence of bi-modal trailers as a realistic alternative to piggyback.

Railcars

The Intermodal Fleet

In 1984 the demands of the international market and the physical characteristics of standard ISO containers played the dominant role in determining intermodal railcar technology. By 1988, the domestic market and the larger domestic containers inspired efforts to modify those original designs. While there was an enormous increase in the doublestack fleet in just four years, only a modest increase in the fleet of new trailer-carrying cars has occurred (Figure 3-1). Furthermore, the fleet of older, unmodified TOFC and COFC cars is dwindling, and a much larger proportion of the total intermodal railcar capacity is now devoted to containers. However, because railcars can remain in service 20 years or more (as compared with five to nine years for piggyback trailers), unconverted piggyback equipment may still be a valuable asset for secondary container service, even if containers eventually supplant piggyback trailers.

The dramatic growth in the doublestack fleet has come from several different sources:

– Cars purchased or leased by ocean carriers

– Cars purchased or leased by railroads, and assigned to ocean carriers

The Rail Intermodal Fleet

| | Total Spaces | 1st/2nd Generation Cars | 3rd Generation | | |
			TOFC Cars	Stack Cars	Road—Railers
1983	110,000	109,000	200	400	300
1984	112,000	109,000	700	2,000	300
1985	119,000	109,000	2,900	7,000	300
1986	118,000	102,000	3,100	13,000	300
1987	116,000	93,000	4,800	18,000	1,400
1988 est.	118,000	88,000	5,800	24,000	2,300

Source: Greenbrier Intermodal

Figure 3-1

61

- Cars purchased or leased by Trailer Train, assigned to railroads, then assigned by the railroads to ocean carriers

- Cars drawn by railroads from a pool of Trailer Train or railroad-owned cars.

The majority of doublestack cars, and the principal source for ocean carriers (other than APC or Sea-Land) have been those purchased or leased by Trailer Train and assigned to railroads or operated in pools. Railroads own or lease only a small number of doublestack cars, and the only steamship lines that have actually purchased or leased cars directly are APC and Sea-Land.

Doublestacks

In one of the many ironies that have occurred in the world of deregulated freight transportation, a steamship line showed the railroads how to make this specific new railcar technology pay off. Despite the fact that the Southern Pacific first operated doublestacks and demonstrated their capabilities as early as 1981, it was American President Lines which actually took the daring step of placing these cars into regularly scheduled unit train service in 1984. Since that time numerous other steamship lines, all major railroads, many other Class I railroads, and even some regional railroads have joined the doublestack parade.

The doublestacks that American President Lines placed into service were five-platform, 40-foot well cars designed by Budd and built by Thrall. A few cars were even built with generator sets to power refrigerated containers. A major feature of these cars was the use of interbox connectors (IBCs)to lock the upper containers in position. Thrall claimed that IBCs would allow faster loading than the ACF/SP bulkhead system.

The Thrall cars were based on the Budd LoPac-2000 design, which was intended to move piggyback trailers through restricted clearances by placing them in a depressed well. The design was adapted for container use by replacing the well floor with container brackets. The lack of bulkheads would become more important later on when 48-foot and 53-foot domestic containers had to be accommodated. Because these longer domestic containers have multiple attachment points (known as corner castings) they could be stacked easily on top of 40-foot and 45-foot containers in IBC cars, but they could not fit within 40-foot or 45-foot bulkheads.

"Twin-Stack" doublestack cars were introduced by FMC in 1984, subsequently built by Gunderson and marketed by Greenbrier Intermodal. Because the Twin-Stacks used bulkheads similar to the ACF/SP design to secure the containers, they had a higher tare weight than the Thrall cars. The first Gunderson cars were delivered to Burlington Northern beginning in 1985 under Greenbrier Leasing's reporting marks. Sea-Land's initial dedicated trains used Gunderson cars with New York, Susquehanna & Western reporting marks. Nearly 4,000 Gunderson cars have been delivered thus far, with Sea-Land, Santa Fe, Burlington Northern, Conrail and Southern Pacific as the main users. The majority are actually owned by Trailer Train.

In 1985, a special, aerodynamically enhanced prototype version of the Twin-Stack bulkhead car was produced. Wind-tunnel tests had shown that the length of

Figure 3-2 This Thrall-built Lopac 2000 IBC double-stack car is being loaded with Maersk containers by a Mi-Jack 90 side-loading "Piggy Packer". Courtesy Thrall Car Manufacturing Company.

Figure 3-3 An early version of Gunderson's "Twin-Stack" bulkhead double-stack car being loaded with sea-land containers. Courtesy Gunderson, Inc.

the gap between containers on adjacent platforms was the most important contributor to aerodynamic drag. In an attempt to mitigate this problem, Gunderson designed and built a Twin-Stack version with vertical metal panels called "barn doors" placed between the upper tier of containers, effectively splitting the long gap between platforms into two smaller gaps that did not interrupt the airstream. The car was ungainly, but aerodynamically effective. The vertical panels interfered with loading and unloading, however, and were actually more counterproductive than beneficial, except when the car was fully loaded. Subsequent bulkhead cars have not had these features.

Trinity's doublestack cars were derived from a Youngstown steel door "Backpacker" prototype, using an IBC design.

As with any successful new technology, enhancements to it were soon to follow. Once the basic design – a five-unit articulated well car with a 100,000 pound capacity per unit – had proved itself, the stack car entered into a period of refinement and improvement. The changes, although significant, were not as dramatic as the original concept itself. "Evolution rather than revolution," is how one car builder described what was happening to stack car technology.

Without a doubt, the two most important stack car refinements were the 125-ton truck and the 48-foot well. Both of these "evolutionary" enhancements to the original stack car design were in direct response to shippers' needs for increased weight and volumetric capacities. Recognizing these needs, all three stack car suppliers – Gunderson, Thrall and Trinity – began producing cars with 125-ton trucks and 48-foot wells, giving each platform of the five-unit cars a weight capacity of approximately 125,000 pounds.

In fact, the marketplace seems to have finally decided on the optimum doublestack design – the five-platform, 125-ton truck, IBC car. These "heavy lift" cars are all able to handle two fully loaded (street legal) containers with a combined total weight of 120,000 to 125,000 pounds on one platform. All cars either currently being produced or being planned for by the doublestack builders fit this description. To be sure, there are some minor variations on the theme, with differing well capacities being offered to accommodate assorted container sizes; but, the basic configuration, at least for now, is established.

Of course, not everyone believes that the bulkhead car has no future. One staunch defender of the bulkhead car design said, "Reports on the death of the bulkhead car, like Mark Twain's death, are greatly exaggerated." Time will tell.

One thing the two leading doublestack manufacturers – Gunderson and Thrall – seem to agree on is that, with 125-ton cars, no extra weight can be allowed. Gunderson acknowledged that when going to the 125-ton car the company needed to save every ounce of car weight it could. Thrall Car concurred with that sentiment by pointing out that bulkheads have unnecessary weight that takes away from the carrying capacity of the car.

The Heavy Lift Contenders

"Maxi-Stack" was Gunderson's first generation heavy-lift, doublestack car. With its 125-ton trucks and

Figure 3-4   One of only ten bulkhead-type 125-ton double-stack cars built by Thrall. Courtesy Thrall Car Manufacturing Company.

non-bulkhead (i.e. IBC) design it is capable of carrying 124,200 pounds on each of its five platforms. The car, which is a shade over 265 feet long, can accommodate one 40-foot or two 20-foot containers within each well, and handle any size containers from 40-foot to 48-foot x 102-inch on the top level. By way of comparison, Gunderson's "Twin-Stack" bulkhead car, which has a similar container carrying configuration and is the same length as the Maxi-Stack, has a tare weight that is approximately 7,000 pounds greater but a per unit weight capacity that is 24,200 pounds less.

To meet the demands of the growing domestic container business Gunderson developed "Maxi-Stack II," its second generation heavy-lift doublestack. Nearly 25 feet longer than its predecessor, Maxi-Stack II has a slightly lower weight capacity of 122,000 pounds per unit, but it can accommodate 40-, 45-, and 48-foot containers in its three intermediate wells. The two end unit wells can hold one 40-foot or two 20-foot containers. On the upper level, the car can carry 40-foot through 48-foot containers on the end units and 40-foot through 53-foot containers on the intermediate units. Gunderson has plans for yet a third generation 125-ton truck, IBC doublestack, "Maxi-Stack III." This new car being built for the Burlington Northern will be able to accommodate 20-, 24- (with 20-foot ISO corner casting locations), 40-, 45-, and 48-foot containers in every well.

Thrall has introduced a heavy-lift version of its highly successful "Lopac 2000" five-unit, IBC double-stack. Known as the "Lopac II," this car comes in two distinct configurations – the 40-foot well and the 40/48-foot well. With its capacity of 120,000 to 122,000 pounds per unit, the 40-foot well car, which is over 267 feet long, can carry one 40-foot or two 20-foot containers in its

Figure 3-5 A Gunderson "Maxi-Stack" 125-ton IBC heavy-lift double-stack car in service with Maersk Lines. Courtesy Gunderson, Inc.

wells and 40-, 45-, or 48-foot containers above.

The 40/48-foot well configuration of the Lopac II is over 291 feet long and has a nominal capacity of 120,500 pounds per unit. The car's two end units can hold one 40-foot or two 20-foot containers on the bottom, topped by one 40-, 45-, 48-, or 53- foot container. The three intermediate units can carry a 40-, 45-, or 48- foot container in the well. The top container on the inter-mediate units can range in size up to 53 feet, but in no case can it be shorter than the bottom one.

Trailer Train and Thrall have looked at another variation of the heavy-lift doublestack: the stand-alone (or single-unit) heavy haul car, of which prototypes have been built. However, Thrall expects little demand for such a car because the 120,000-plus pound per unit capacity of existing heavy-lift articulated doublestacks can handle most current domestic loads. Thrall believes that unless highway load limits are substantially increased it is unlikely there will ever be a real need for the stand-alone cars.

Trinity also offered a single-unit version of its "Backpacker" IBC car, but that company, too, has not seen much interest in the car.

DoubleStack Comparisons

Features and specifications of nine different double-stack cars built by ACF, Gunderson, Thrall and Trinity, and the Trinity-built spine car are given for comparison in Figure 3-8. Several observations are immediately apparent:

71

Figure 3-6   Thrall-built "Lopac II" 125-ton IBC heavy-lift double-stack car being loaded with APL containers. Courtesy Thrall Car Manufacturing Company.

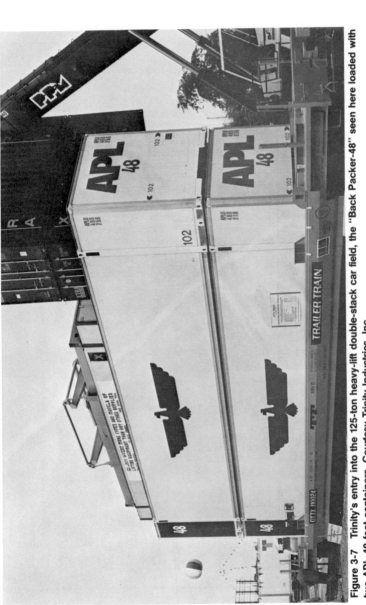

Figure 3-7 Trinity's entry into the 125-ton heavy-lift double-stack car field, the "Back Packer-48" seen here loaded with two APL 48-foot containers. Courtesy Trinity Industries, Inc.

Double-Stack Cars

Car	Type	Well[1] Length	Top[1] Length	Overall Length	Avg. Platform Tare	Avg. Platform Net	Net/Tare
ACF/SP	Bulkhead	35/40	35/40	265–2	39,400	94,000	2.39
Lopac 2000	IBC	40/40	40/45	266–2	30,700	102,800	3.35
Lopac II	IBC	40/48	40/53	288–10	38,000	120,500	3.17
Twin–Stack	Bulkhead	40/40	40/45	265–2	34,600	100,000	2.89
Maxi–Stack	IBC	40/40	40/48	265–2	35,400	124,200	3.51
Maxi–Stack II	IBC	40/48	40/53	289–8	36,800	122,000	3.32
Backpacker	IBC	40/40	40/48	264–7	32,400	102,500	3.16
Backpacker–48	IBC	40/48	40/53	288–7	37,000[2]	120,000[2]	3.24
Backpacker–Single	IBC	48	48/53	64–0	42,000	145,600[2,3]	2.79
Spine Car	Pedestal	48	–/–	249–0	26,120	72,800[2,3]	3.47

1 – End/Center well lengths, Nominal/Maximum top lengths
2 – Estimated
3 – Limited by gross container weight

74

- Bulkhead cars (ACF and Gunderson Twin-Stacks) have higher tare weight than IBC cars.

- The capability of carrying longer containers increases with overall car length, up to a point (the capability of placing a 53-foot container on the upper tier of an IBC car results in no additional length penalty).

- All of the current doublestack designs have substantial tare weight advantages over the spine car.

The specifications also indicate that the latest generation of stack cars offered by the three active builders are very similar. The Thrall LoPac II 40/48, the Gunderson Maxi-Stack II and Trinity Backpacker-48 are all approximately 290 feet long, weigh 36,000 to 38,000 pounds per platform and can accommodate 48- and 53-foot containers.

Spine and Skeleton Container Cars

Union Pacific was the first railroad to build a modern articulated, single-stack "skeleton" car for containers. The car, introduced in 1983, weighed 45 tons and consisted of five units each shaped like a capital "I" to support the containers at their corners.

The multi-platform single-stack container cars currently in wide use are Trailer Train's "Spine Cars." These come in two designs, one from Trinity and the other from Bethlehem Steel. Introduced in 1987, both designs can handle up to five 48-foot containers, with the capability of carrying 20-foot containers on every other platform.

Figure 3-9 A five-unit articulated spine car designed to carry single-stack containers. Courtesy Trailer Train.

In January 1989 Trailer Train announced the development of a new type of articulated, lightweight, five-unit flatcar that can carry both containers and piggyback trailers. Known as the "All-Purpose Spine Car," it represents an important refinement to the design of earlier lightweight, articulated flatcars, which were capable of carrying either containers or trailers, but not both.

Trailers carried on the All-Purpose Spine Car will range in length from 28 to 48 feet and containers will range from 20 to 48 feet. The car, which is expected to weigh 165,000 pounds, will have such features as conventional three-piece 70-ton trucks, non-cushioned retractable hitches and automatic locking devices to engage container corner castings.

Trailer Train has also begun work on another all-purpose car design based on its "Front Runner" lightweight, single-axle TOFC car first introduced in 1983. This all-purpose car will have two Front Runners permanently coupled together by a drawbar and will be capable of carrying 48-foot trailers or 20- through 48-foot containers.

Spine and skeleton cars offer more in the way of flexibility than stack cars, especially since stack car economics demand intensive utilization and heavy traffic volumes. Compared to doublestacks, spine cars have a lower capital cost, and could provide satisfactory economics when less intensively used. In this sense, they might be seen as a replacement for conventional flatcars. Spine cars can also be used on routes where there is insufficient bridge or tunnel clearance for stack car trains and could also provide a low cost means of developing a feeder network to complement a doublestack system.

Intermodal Flatcars

For many years the workhorse of intermodal rail equipment has been the flatcar. From the first time a trailer was placed atop one for a piggyback move until very recently, the conventional intermodal flatcar has been the mainstay of rail intermodal operations. Despite inroads from stack cars, spine cars, bi-modal trailers and the like, flatcars are likely to remain an important part of the intermodal scene for a long time to come.

Until the advent of mechanized lift equipment, TOFC trailers were usually "circus loaded." Circus loading was accomplished by positioning TOFC flatcars end-on to a sloping ramp, lowering bridgeplates to form a continuous driveable surface over the cars, and backing trailers up the ramp and into position, one at a time. The name came from the longstanding practice of loading circus wagons the same way. When it was the dominant loading method, TOFC flatcars had to be equipped with collapsible hitches and moveable bridgeplates, both of which caused maintenance problems for railroads. By today's standards, circus loading is an inefficient, obsolete technology, and has virtually disappeared.

During the 1950s, general purpose 50-foot flatcars were used extensively for TOFC service. Today, specialized intermodal flatcars come in several lengths and configurations. The most prominent is the 89-foot flat, which, depending on how it is configured, can carry two 45-foot or shorter trailers, or three 28-foot trailers, or a mix of 20-, 40-, and 45- foot containers. The less common 85-foot flat can carry four 20-foot or two 40-

foot containers. There is also a 60-foot flat that can handle either three 20-foot or one 20-foot and one 40-foot container.

The majority of the intermodal flatcars in service today are owned by Trailer Train and are either "free-running" or assigned to specific railroads. Trailer Train has done much to improve intermodal flatcar technology. In 1980 the company initiated its "Twin-45" program of modifying 89-foot flatcars to accommodate two 45-foot trailers, as these longer trailers began to replace 40-foot units. Three years later Trailer Train introduced the "Front Runner," a 50-foot, light-weight, single-axle skeleton TOFC car capable of carrying one 40-, 45-, or 48-foot trailer. Since their introduction in 1983, about 2,800 Front Runners have been built.

More recently, in response to the need for handling multiple trailers of lengths 48 feet or greater, Trailer Train developed the "Long Runner." Taking two existing 89-foot flatcars and hitching them together with a permanent one-piece drawbar, Trailer Train engineers created a new intermodal car with the capacity to carry four 45-foot, or three 48-foot, or three 53- foot, or even three 57-foot trailers. Trailer Train has thus found one way to meet the challenge of ever-lengthening trailers.

Finally, the "all-purpose" flatcars combine container and trailer capability. Trailer Train's all-purpose TTAX flatcars were designed and built with bridgeplates, collapsible hitches and retractable container pedestals to accommodate either trailers or containers. Although these cars were useful because of their ability to accommodate both types of intermodal traffic, the process of changing configurations was time-consuming and the greater number of moving parts added to mainte-

Figure 3-10 A 50-foot "TTX" TOFC flat car loaded with a 40-foot MOPAC trailer. Courtesy Trailer Train.

Figure 3-11   A 75-foot two-hitch TOFC. The only flat car built in 1957. It was designed to accommodate two trailers up to 35 feet long. Courtesy Trailer Train.

Figure 3-12   A "GTTX" TOFC car built by General American Car in 1961. It had "Knock-Down" hitches and could carry two 40-foot trailers. Courtesy Trailer Train

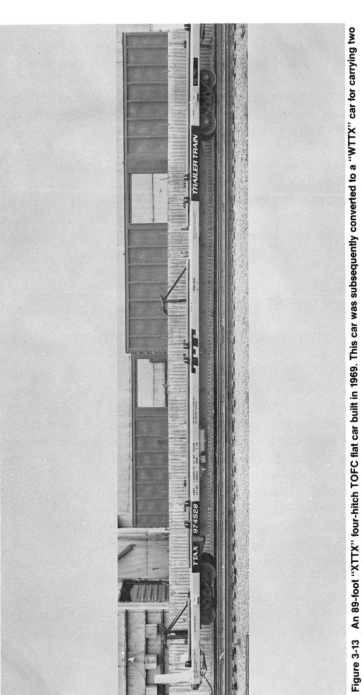

Figure 3-13 An 89-foot "XTTX" four-hitch TOFC flat car built in 1969. This car was subsequently converted to a "WTTX" car for carrying two 45-foot trailers. Courtesy Trailer Train.

nance requirements. By 1988, Trailer Train removed the bridgeplates from these cars and modified the hitches to allow two 45-foot trailers or containers on chassis.

It is interesting to note that neither of Trailer Train's new all-purpose cars (the All Purpose Spine Car and the Front Runner-based design) will carry 53-foot containers. According to Trailer Train planners, they made a conscious decision not to accommodate 53-foot containers on either of the new cars. The feeling at Trailer Train was that, for the time being, the market for cars to handle 53-foot containers is too small and the cost of building such cars is too high. Evidently there is enough space on the upper tier of the doublestack fleet to accommodate foreseeable 53-foot container requirements.

Skeleton Trailer Cars

Although Trailer Train's conversion and upgrade efforts have greatly extended the life of the intermodal flatcar fleet, Santa Fe, long a leader in TOFC service, has led a movement towards skeletonized, articulated cars for trailers. The Santa Fe cars, which were initially named "Six Packs," then "Ten Packs," and now "Fuel Foilers," are essentially an articulated series of center sills with trailer hitches and abbreviated platforms for trailer wheels. The object and the result were lighter tare weight, improved aerodynamics and a smoother ride. Santa Fe built the original cars for its own on-line use. However, Itel purchased the rights to the design, and now produces its own version known as the "Impack" car for interchange use. Trailer Train and other railroads have purchased a number of Impack cars, but Santa Fe remains the predominant user.

Figure 3-14 The all purpose "TTAX" 89-foot flat car built in 1974 to carry both trailers and containers and later converted to carry two 45-foot trailers. Nearly 15,000 are still in service. Courtesy Trailer Train.

Figure 3-15 An Itel "Impack" skeleton trailer car being loaded with Burlington Northern trailers. Courtesy Itel Rail Corporation.

Thrall has developed two lightweight, articulated TOFC cars, the "ARC-5" and the "ARC-3", for the piggyback market. Similar in appearance to Impack cars, these are skeleton trailer cars with cushioned hitches and small platforms long enough to accommodate the trailer bogies. The ARC-5 is a five-unit car that can carry 40-, 45-, and 48-foot trailers. The ARC-3 is a three-unit car that can carry 40- and 45-foot trailers.

Trailer-Railer

The doublestack car, of course, is not the only innovative rail intermodal technology that has come along lately. In 1988, Trailer-Rail, Inc. of Chicago developed and tested a unique new intermodal railcar, the Trailer-Railer. This drop-deck car with two single-axle trucks has a tare weight of about 22,000 pounds and is only 23 1/2 feet long. Used in pairs, these unusual railcars act as bogies to carry standard highway trailers ranging in length from 28 to 60 feet. Containers can be handled on chassis, or 20-foot containers can be placed directly on the cars.

A trailer is loaded by backing it up an inclined side ramp and onto the first car's drop-deck platform where the trailer wheels are locked in place by adjustable chocks. The front of the trailer is then swung over and its kingpin is connected to the trailer hitch on the adjacent Trailer-Railer. Thus the trailer "bridges" the two Trailer-Railers and, in effect, becomes part of the railcar itself. The entire loading operation takes approximately 10 minutes and requires no special lift equipment.

The Iowa Interstate Railroad, a participant in the

Trailer-Railer program, completed successful testing of two prototype Trailer-Railers in 1988. Yard tests were performed first to evaluate the loading and unloading characteristics of the cars. After completion of the yard tests, the prototypes were taken on the road to simulate running conditions with a trailing load.

Plans call for operating Trailer-Railers in unit trains pulling up to 15 trailers each with a total trailing load of 600 to 650 tons. The Iowa Interstate sees an application for Trailer-Railers not only with other regionals, but on the Class I carriers as well, particularly those with no intermodal equipment to handle trailers longer than 45 feet.

Because of its relatively low capital requirements for both equipment and terminal facilities, as well as its low operating costs, the Trailer-Railer system could prove to be very effective in competing against trucks in the short haul market of 500 miles or less, where a great majority of intercity freight traffic now moves. In fact, Trailer-Rail estimates that the capital and operating costs for a Trailer-Railer service could be as little as half those for a conventional intermodal operation of comparable capacity.

Carless Technology

Carless technology, which combines the two transportation modes of rail and truck into one, seeks to maximize rail line-haul efficiency by eliminating, or at least minimizing, the railcar itself. This approach may yield additional benefits in the ease of loading and unloading, and in minimizing the need for facility investment.

RoadRailer®

RoadRailer®, in its various forms, is the most common carless technology and the only one that has seen commercial application.

After some years of design work and prototype construction, production of RoadRailers® began with the Mark IV 45-foot dry van model in 1981. The Mark IV RoadRailer® is basically a highway trailer that also carries retractable rail wheels. The original RoadRailer® design placed the rail wheels at the extreme rear, behind the highway wheels. For operational reasons the design was changed to place the rail wheels between the two highway axles. An air suspension system is used to change from highway to rail mode, and the RoadRailer® carries both highway and rail compatible air brake systems. Because the RoadRailer® is intended to operate in trains of 75 or more units, the frame is strengthened to handle the drawbar pull.

On the rails, each RoadRailer® is attached to the unit in front, without the benefit of additional wheels. Each unit thus supports a portion of its own weight, and a portion of the unit behind. In order to couple with standard locomotives, the first unit in each train must be a special AdaptaRailer. Mark IV RoadRailers® can be positioned on the tracks by a yard tractor, eliminating the need for ordinary railroad switching.

Minor modifications to the original design of Road-Railers® have been made. By increasing the brake line diameter for example, RoadRailer® has been successful in achieving sufficient braking to support a 100-unit train. RoadRailer® Mark IV 48-foot x 102-inch units also successfully withstood a compressive force of 500,000 pounds (25% above design specifications) in squeeze tests conducted late in 1987, another factor indicating RoadRailer® trains will be of increased length in the future.

Other modifications include a "highway lockout" system designed to prevent damage to the rail wheels caused by dragging on the pavement. The device locks the highway brakes until the vehicle achieves sufficient ride height to ensure the rail wheels are clear of the road.

In 1986, the Mark V RoadRailer® was introduced. In the Mark V system, the rail wheels take the form of a detachable bogie equipped with brackets to hold the trailer body and a rail brake system. Besides reducing the cost and mechanical complexity of the RoadRailer® trailer, this change also significantly reduced the tare weight and increased the highway payload. Because the rail bogie remains with the railroad, each bogie can serve more than one trailer body. The currently accepted ratio is 175 trailers per 100 bogies. Trailer Train has recently begun to participate in the supply of bogies. Present versions of the Mark V have reached 53 feet in length, with a 96-inch door width.

The primary advantages of RoadRailers® are the reductions in tare weight compared to TOFC technology, the elimination of a separate chassis, the reduction in investment for railcars (although the Mark V requires an investment in bogies),and greatly reduced facility cost. RoadRailers® themselves are expensive, however, relative to trailers – roughly $50,000 versus $15,000. This greater capital expense creates problems with railroad control over equipment that leaves the property, since utilization becomes critical. RoadRailers® are also at a tare weight disadvantage relative to trailers, although the

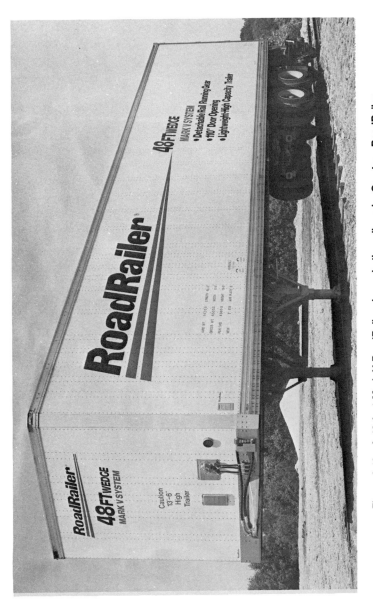

Figure 3-16 A 48-foot Mark V RoadRailer shown in the rail mode. Courtesy RoadRailer.

91

Mark V version narrows the gap.

With well over 2,000 RoadRailer® trailers built to date, most of which are still in service, RoadRailer® has clearly demonstrated the viability of its carless technology. The company's product line includes these different pieces of RoadRailer® equipment:

– The 48-foot Mark IV System (permanently installed single-axle rail bogie) Dry Van with a 3,455 cubic foot capacity.

– The 48-foot Mark V System (detachable twin-axle rail bogie) Wedge Dry Van with a 3,529 cubic foot capacity.

– The 53-foot Mark V System Super Wedge Trailer with a 3,930 cubic foot capacity.

– The 48-foot x 102-inch Mark V System RefrigerRailer (refrigerated) Trailer with 3,136 cubic foot capacity.

– The 40-foot Mark V System ContainerRailer (container chassis) Trailer capable of carrying one 40-foot x 96-inch ISO container.

– The 40-foot Mark V System DumpRailer (dump trailer) with a 52 cubic yard capacity.

Each piece of RoadRailer® equipment is fully compatible with all other models of Mark IV and Mark V trailers and may be intermixed within a train.

Apart from the high cost of bi-modal trailer equipment, another block to their widespread use may lie in

Figure 3-17 The RoadRailer Mark V "Dump Railer" in the process of being transferred to the rail mode by a standard highway tractor. Courtesy RoadRailer.

their comparative inflexibility. The overall strength of the trailer units is not sufficient to withstand the compressive forces typical in ordinary trains. As a result, bi-modal units cannot be run with conventional types of railcars. For this and other reasons, RoadRailers® in revenue service have only been operated as distinct unit trains. However, to explore the feasibility of operating RoadRailers® behind doublestack trains, tests were conducted under the sponsorship of the Burlington Northern at the Transportation Test Center in the fall of 1988. As many as 40 trailers, both Mark IVs and Mark Vs, were coupled to a doublestack car using a special hitch designed jointly by BN and Gunderson.

BN was encouraged by the results of the tests, which indicated that the two technologies can be combined. The ride quality and fuel economy of articulated doublestack cars do make them a logical choice to combine with RoadRailers®. BN plans to ask the Federal Railroad Administration for a waiver to use combined doublestack/RoadRailer® trains in revenue service.

Other Carless Technologies

In the absence of any other operational models, market sales of bi-modal trailers have been exclusively RoadRailer® equipment. However, there is serious competition to RoadRailer® in the carless technology market. Until Strick introduced its prototype RailTrailer at the International Intermodal Expo at Atlanta in April 1988, the only other entry RoadRailer® had to face was from Railmaster, but RoadRailer® acquired Railmaster taking the detachable truck idea and offering it as the Mark V RoadRailer®. But now it faces a new challenge from the old line trailer manufacturer and its joint venture partner

94

Sambre et Meuse, which, as the largest steel foundry in France, has over 100 years' experience in railcar castings and truck design.

Strick developed the RailTrailer at the request of at least two Class I railroads. The RailTrailer design differs most notably from RoadRailer® in that it utilizes aperture openings in the lower front and rear corners of the trailer with dimensions and spacings that match the configuration of standard ISO corner castings. The apertures on the trailers connect to twist locks attached to bolsters mounted on rail bogies. Train forces are distributed between the bottom rails of the trailer through the bogies. Unlike the RoadRailer® system, which uses a rail bogie attached at or near the back end of each trailer, each RailTrailer shares a bogie at its front and back with the adjacent RailTrailers.

Strick plans to make RailTrailer trailers available in all sizes, ranging from 28-foot x 102-inch to 53-foot x 102-inch, each with a full 110-inch rear door opening. The standard twist lock configuration will also allow the use of existing containers with the RailTrailer bogies, provided the containers meet minimum strength requirements. As with the trailers, any length container can be accommodated. Strick believes that the RailTrailer system, with its lighter weight components, greater capacity and reduced terminal handling requirements, will offer operators substantial cost savings and greater operational efficiency. Because of its basically slackless action, the RailTrailer system should provide the same high quality ride that is available with doublestack trains and Road-Railer® trains.

Strick began building production models in 1989. The company completed private line testing of four

Strick Prototype RailTrailers undergoing testing.

**Close-up of RailTrailer Bogie Assembly. Courtesy
Strick Intermodal.**

Figure 3-18

prototype trailers with four bogies on the Santa Fe in the fall of 1988 and made plans to perform more extensive testing at the Transportation Test Center in Pueblo, CO. Strick was encouraged by test results, particularly in the stability and overall performance of the trailers.

As for the concern about incompatibility between the RoadRailer® system and the RailTrailer system, Strick views this as a railroad issue. From Strick's point of view, it would be easy to develop a method of running blocks of the two different carless designs on the same train, if that is what a railroad wanted. However, the company feels that doing this is really more a commercial than a technology matter.

Fastrack Freightways has also been developing a bi-modal trailer design, but has yet to produce a prototype. According to the company, there will be key differences between the "Fastracker" unit and RoadRailer®. Fastrack Freightways intends to produce only a detachable bogie system and there will be no Mark IV equivalent. More important, however, Fastracker units will utilize new "air-ride" suspension systems instead of the conventional steel springs used in RoadRailer®. Apart from the difference in ride quality, air suspension allows the detachable bogie to sit deflated on the rail track below the clearance level of the trailer. The trailer would be positioned over the bogie without the use of lift equipment, then raised into position when the bogie suspension is inflated, much like an air-operated jack.

Fastrack is optimistic about the potential success of the Fastracker, perhaps for good reason. For one, the railroad community is unlikely to want to rely on a sole supplier for bi-modal equipment and for another, there is potentially more than enough room for two or even more carless technology manufacturers.

Despite some limitations, bi-modal trailers can be competitive with motor carrier service in certain corridors. No specialized lift equipment is needed, so they can be run out of small terminals and can deliver door-to-door. RoadRailer® estimates the break-even mileage is between 400-500 miles and, above that, RoadRailer® becomes more competitive than motor carriers. For these reasons, the overall future for bi-modal trailers seems encouraging.

Piggyback Trailers

Compared to the nation's highway fleet, the present piggyback fleet is a collection of old, and undersized trailers. In 1988 it was estimated that approximately 62% of all piggyback trailers were over nine years old, and these older units were all of the 40-foot x 96-inch or 45-foot x 96-inch variety. To be sure, there were some younger (three years or less) pigs of the 45-foot x 102-inch and 48-foot x 102-inch variety, but these represented less than 40% of the fleet. The news was not all bad however, because trailer industry analysts predict that by 1993 73% of the piggyback fleet would be composed of the larger-size trailers less than five years old, indicating that TOFC service may be making a recovery.

Equipment suppliers, too, are optimistic about the future of piggyback trailers. The Monon Corporation of Monon, Ind., reported that it had plans to build nearly 2,000 45-foot x 102-inch TOFC trailers in 1989. This represented approximately 60% of Monon's planned intermodal equipment construction. Monon believed most emphatically that the TOFC trailer market was not dead.

Another leading trailer manufacturer, Stoughton Trailers of Stoughton, Wis., also felt that the piggyback market was still strong. In 1989, Stoughton planned to build approximately 60 45-foot x 102-inch "high-cube" (i.e., 110-inch height throughout) TOFC trailers each week. Stoughton has been heavily involved in the intermodal equipment business, including the construction of 300 RoadRailer® trailers in 1988. The company estimated that at least half of its 6,000 units planned for 1989 were for the intermodal market.

Fruehauf Trailer Operations in Middletown, Penn., reported that it built several thousand 48-foot piggyback trailers in 1988. As for 1989, Fruehauf anticipated that a total of at least 8,000 TOFC trailers would be constructed at its facilities nationwide.

Containers

ISO Standard Containers

ISO standard containers come in a wide variety of sizes, ranging from 10 to 45 feet, and in a wide variety of types, from the more commonplace "dry van" to the more exotic tank container. According to the ISO definition, a freight container is an "article of transport equipment" that meets the following requirements:

- It is of permanent character and strong enough for repeated use.

- It is specifically designed for transporting goods by more than one mode without intermediate reloading.

– It has fittings that permit easy handling when being transferred from one mode to another.

– It is designed for easy filling and emptying.

– It has an internal volume greater than one cubic meter.

The ISO definition specifically excludes vehicles and conventional packaging.

Series 1 containers are those ISO standard containers intended for intercontinental use and consequently must be built to endure the rigors of shipboard service. By far and away, the most commonly seen containers on US highways and railroads are 20-foot and 40-foot ISO Series 1 containers, despite the recent introduction of purely domestic containers. In 1988, the worldwide fleet of freight containers of all types was estimated to be nearly 5 million units.

ISO standards describe over 20 different types of containers that are divided into two broad groups – general cargo containers and specific cargo containers. As the names imply, general cargo containers are those not intended to carry some particular category of cargo and specific cargo containers are those intended for cargos that require temperature control, for liquids and gases, for dry bulk solids, and for items such as automobiles and livestock. From a physical appearance perspective, containers can be broken into three very general types: boxes, platforms, and tanks. Within each of these three categories, there are several sub-categories.

The most prevalent box is the general purpose container or "dry van," which is totally enclosed and weatherproof, has a rigid roof, rigid floor, rigid side walls and rigid end walls, has doors in at least one end wall, and is suitable for carrying the greatest possible variety of cargo.

Other types of boxes include:

– Ventilated containers with ventilation systems designed to increase the natural flow of air through the inside of the container

– Vented containers with passive vents near the upper parts

– Open top containers without a rigid roof

– Thermal containers with insulated walls, roof and floor to retard the flow of heat between the inside and outside

– Refrigerated thermal containers with expendable refrigerant that requires no external power

– Mechanically refrigerated thermal containers with a refrigerating appliance

– Heated thermal containers with a heat-producing appliance

– Refrigerated and heated thermal containers with both refrigeration and heat-producing appliances

Platform containers or "flatracks" are used to carry oversized and odd-shaped cargo that cannot fit easily into a box, such as machinery and earth moving equipment. These versatile containers, which come in the same width and length (usually 20- foot or 40-foot) as the base of standard box containers and have corner castings at the same standard locations, are available in several versions. Besides the basic platform container with no superstructure whatsoever, there are also platforms with fixed end walls, platforms with folding (collapsible) end walls, platforms with folding end posts (legs) and platforms with folding headframes. Empty platforms that have no end walls or that have collapsible end walls, posts and headframes can be stacked and locked together into "modules" of standard ISO dimensions for shipment.

Tank containers are simply tanks securely enclosed within a structural steel framework that meets standard ISO dimensions. There are also dry bulk tank containers (very similar in appearance to liquid-carrying tank containers) that are used for hauling a variety of dry bulk solids. Because of the weight of the products involved, the maximum allowable capacity of both liquid and dry bulk tank containers limits their length to 20 feet.

A common sight in Europe for many years, tank containers are slowly gaining acceptance in the US. Recent growth trends in the American chemical industry should fuel US demand for these highly versatile containers as foreign markets expand. The total number of tank containers worldwide was estimated at just over 25,000 in 1988; however, this number was expected to grow substantially as more liquid and dry bulk shippers recognize their benefits.

Figure 3-19 A rather unique flatrack, this "extendable" flatrack can be lengthened from the standard 20-foot size to 22 feet, 24 feet or 26 feet.

Figure 3-20 Typical 20-foot ISO tank container. Courtesy International Container Leasing Limited.

When compared with shipping in 55 gallon drums, tank containers are definitely superior. A typical 20-foot tank container with its capacity of 4,800-6,600 gallons can hold 800-2,250 gallons more product than the 72-80 drums that can be stowed in a 20-foot box container of the same outside dimensions. Consequently, in an equal amount of space aboard a ship or on a railcar, a tank container can move between 20% to 66% more materials than drums in a box container.

Domestic Containers

Domestic containers are those containers built exclusively for domestic use in the US. These generally include 45-foot, 48-foot, and 53-foot high-cube (102-inch wide x 9 1/2-foot high) dry vans that are intended for rail and highway service only, although 45-foot boxes built to ISO standards are occasionally also used aboard ship. APC, one of the intermodal leaders, introduced 48-foot containers to the domestic scene in 1985 and then followed up with the first 53-foot containers in 1988.

Since domestic containers are not meant for international shipments, there is no requirement to build them to ISO standards. They all do, however, have standard ISO corner castings located at the 40-foot positions on both the top and bottom to permit stacking with standard 40-foot containers. Despite their greater volumetric capacity, the gross weight of domestic containers is usually limited to 67,200 pounds, the same as that for standard ISO 40-foot container.

One of the most significant domestic container developments in 1988 occurred when the "domestic" in

Figure 3-21 An American President Companies' 53-foot domestic container pioneered by the company for use in certain corridors in North America. Courtesy American President Companies.

domestic container took on two meanings – domestic use and domestic built. Containers were actually being made once again in the US. As many as three US trailer manufacturers were in the domestic container business by 1989 – Monon, Stoughton and Fruehauf.

In 1988 Monon built over 6,000 45-, 48-, and 53-foot domestic containers, all of the 102-inch width variety. Monon also produced 4,600 chassis in 1988 to help haul around some of those containers.

In 1989, Stoughton planned to have one production line dedicated to domestic containers throughout the year. With orders for 2,500 in 1989, this line was expected to turn out 65 to 70 48-foot x 9-foot 6-inch x 102-inch hi-cube domestic boxes each week.

Fruehauf began delivery of 1,000 48-foot x 102-inch domestic containers in 1988. In addition to the domestic boxes, Fruehauf also was producing a small quantity of 20-foot and 40-foot ISO reefer containers in 1988, and had orders for more reefer containers in 1989.

Container Handling Equipment

With the introduction of freight containers into both the international and domestic transportation networks in the late 1950s, the need for specialized equipment to handle them soon became apparent. In those early days of containerization carriers had to make do with cranes, hoists and trailers originally designed for non-containerized cargo. However, as usually occurs in cases where there is a need, someone will fill it. Today, now that most of the international transportation of non-bulk commodities is accomplished using containers, there are numerous manufacturers in Europe, Asia and North America of cranes, hoists, packers and chassis specifically designed from the ground up to lift and move containers.

Dockside Cranes

Early containerships had their own onboard cranes to load and unload containers, since most ports in the early 1960s did not have container cranes. This arrangement became less suitable as containers increased in size, weight and numbers. The more progressive ports soon recognized the necessity to adapt to the new technology and acquired suitable dockside cranes. Steamship lines also began to acquire cranes for their own dock facilities. Today, every major seaport in the world that serves containerships has at least one or more dockside cranes specifically designed for loading and unloading containers.

Early dockside cranes used to handle containers were the hinged-boom type. The crane's cable was usually attached to a rectangular lifting frame that had approximately the same width and length dimensions as a container. A container hook was suspended from each of the four corners of the lifting frame. To lift a container, all four hooks had to be inserted into the top corner castings of the container. The standard ISO corner casting still has an opening on its side through which a hook can be inserted, although this type of lifting is rarely done anymore.

Dockside boom cranes have now largely been replaced by gantry cranes. Built much like a cantilever bridge, the gantry crane is supported by two vertical

Figure 3-22 In this early container loading operation the SS <u>Hawaiian Merchant</u> is being readied for the first Pacific container ship voyage in August 1958. Courtesy Matson Lines

Figure 3-23 This $6 million dockside gantry crane at the Port of Oakland, California is higher than a ten-story building and can lift 50-ton containers at a rate of 50 per hour. Courtesy Port of Oakland.

trestles and has a long horizontal boom which extends out over the containerships. The cranes are usually rail-mounted so that they can move along the dock parallel to the edge. The lifting frame has been replaced by the "spreader," which is suspended from the crane's boom by the hoisting cables. Instead of having hooks on each of its four corners, the spreader has "twistlocks" that are inserted into the top corner castings of the container and rotated to lock into place. Once the container is properly engaged by the spreader, the container can be lifted. Modern spreaders are "telescopic" to adjust to different container lengths and have self-leveling devices to keep the containers on an even keel while they are being hoisted.

Container gantry cranes are massive structures, particularly the ones that have been built to load and unload the new generation of post-Panamax ships. Some of these newest cranes have an outreach over the water of 150 feet, a lifting height of over 100 feet and a lifting capacity greater than 50 tons.

Mobile Container Handling Equipment

A large assortment of mobile equipment for moving, stacking and lifting containers in terminals and container yards has been developed since the beginning of the intermodal revolution. Many of these machines perform the exact or similar function (e.g., lifting containers onto or off of railcars), using different designs and configurations. They are known by a variety of names, including: stackers, packers, frontlift trucks, side loaders, straddle carriers, and stacking gantry cranes. For simplicity's sake, mobile container handling equipment can be divided into two distinct categories – machines that approach

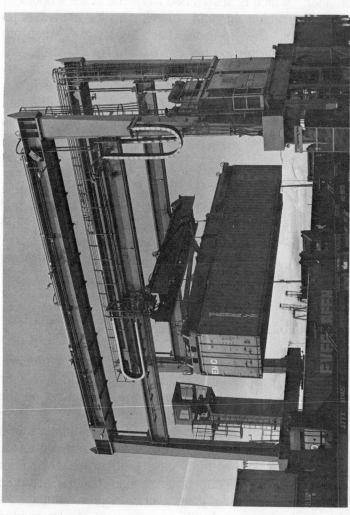

Figure 3-24 A Mi-Jack "Translift" rubber-tired international gantry crane in service with the Burlington Northern Railroad. Courtesy Mi-Jack Products.

Figure 3-25 A Marathon LeTourneau SST-100 "Straddle Hoist" rubber-tired gantry crane. Courtesy Marathon LeTourneau.

Figure 3-26   This Taylor TYC-920L side-loading container handler has a capacity of 70,000 pounds. Courtesy Taylor Machine Works.

Figure 3-27 This Taylor TEC-155L empty container handler is capable of stacking empties five-high. Courtesy Taylor Machine Works

115

containers or trailers from the side and machines that move over the top of, or straddle, them. Within these two categories, there are many various subcategories.

Machines in both categories may have spreaders similar to those used on dockside gantry cranes to lift containers from the top, or they may have grapple arms to lift them from the bottom. In some cases they may have both, the twist locks on the spreader normally being used for containers and the grapple arms being used for trailers. Forklift trucks are used to lift containers fitted with forklift pockets. Some of the machines can perform multiple tasks, such as stacking containers for storage and loading to and from both railcars and chassis, while others may only be used to stack empty containers.

Chassis

A chassis is nothing more than a trailer designed specifically to haul containers. It is basically a skeletal frame platform equipped with twistlocks to secure the container, a bogie assembly, landing gear, a kingpin, and necessary electrical and pneumatic devices. While most chassis are built for over-the-road use, some are intended strictly for use within container yards and terminals.

As with other intermodal equipment, chassis come in a variety of sizes and types, including:

– Chassis for 20-foot containers only.

– Chassis for 40-foot containers only.

– Extendable chassis to accommodate different length containers.

- "Gooseneck" chassis for hi-cube containers.

- "Dropframe" chassis for tank containers.

- "Slider" chassis with bogies that can be re-positioned to adjust the weight distribution.

- Tilt chassis that can dump loads.

The main differences between highway chassis and yard chassis (also called "bomb carts") are that highway chassis must have brakes, lights and licenses for use over public roads, and employ a twistlock chassis securement system, while yard chassis do not need highway safety equipment and employ simple corner brackets to hold the container in place.

Chapter 4

INTERMODAL OPERATIONS

Doublestack Services

Early Rail Container Service

Containers of various kinds are not new to the railroads, or to trucking or maritime shipping. Since the 19th century, there have been numerous attempts to introduce standardized containers for various commodities. Railroad efforts were focused mainly on improved methods for handling Less-than-Carload (LCL) freight. Until the late 1950s, however, none of these attempts resulted in widespread or long-lasting use of containers. In ocean transportation, containerization began in the late 1950s with the efforts of Sea-Land on the East Coast and Matson on the West Coast. Originally, Sea-Land used 35-foot containers in US and European trades while Matson introduced 24-foot containers in the Hawaiian trade.

The success of these ventures and the beginnings of containerization by other ocean carriers led to a crucial step: the standardization of containers by the ISO. After much debate, the ISO issued standards for container sizes and configurations, and for the exact nature of corner castings to serve as securement and lifting points. With standardized container contact points, mechanized lifting machines and rail cars could be designed and built to handle all standard containers.

The initial ISO standards covered containers measuring 8 feet high by 8 feet wide in 20-foot and 40-foot lengths. Later, standards were issued to cover containers measuring 8 feet 6 inches, 9 feet, and 9 feet 6 inches high "high – cube"), and 45-foot long containers. Proposed standards for a longer "wide body" container (9 feet high, 8 feet 6 inches wide) are now under consideration. ISO standard configurations for flat, bulkhead, tank, and other specialized containers have also been established.

The next major development was the introduction of regular marine container movements via rail by SeaTrain in 1972. This event began the expansion of landbridge, mini-landbridge and micro-landbridge services which continues to this day. These services can be described as follows:

Landbridge. A port-to-port movement of containers replacing the middle portion of an ocean voyage that began before the first port and extends beyond the second. For example, a long voyage between Asia and Europe might be replaced by a shorter voyage between Asia and the US West Coast, a landbridge movement between the West and East Coasts, and a final ocean segment between the East Coast and Europe.

Mini-landbridge. A port-to-port movement replacing one end of an ocean voyage. Mini-landbridge (MLB) service uses a land transportation mode – sometimes truck, but usually rail – to serve a second port from a single port call. A good example is an ocean carrier calling at Los Angeles and offering MLB service to and from Houston, rather than calling at Houston directly. Ocean carriers frequently include MLB departures and arrivals in published ship schedules.

Micro-landbridge. Micro-landbridge service operates between a US port of call and an inland US intermodal hub (which may or may not also be a port). Service between Charleston and Atlanta is one example. Chicago is the single largest inland hub for micro-landbridge service.

Inland Points Intermodal. The difference between mini-landbridge and micro-landbridge has little day-to-day significance. The term "Inland Points Intermodal" (IPI) is used by some carriers to denote all inland intermodal services offered under an ocean carrier bill of lading. IPI services are distinguished from Overland Common Point (OCP) services by this simple bill of lading. OCP services use an ocean carrier bill of lading between ports, and a shipper or third party bill of lading inland.

With few exceptions, initial pickup or final delivery of the container is made by truck. The intermodal system depends initially on motor carriers to transfer or "dray" containers between port terminals and nearby rail terminals (except for some on-dock rail terminals, where the drayage has been internalized). The system again depends on motor carriers to make the link between intermodal hubs and the ultimate shipper or consignee. In fact, the concentration of rail intermodal operations at a relatively small number of major hubs has been made possible by the ability of motor carriers to feed those hubs efficiently from distances of up to 250 miles, and sometimes more.

The dedicated unit trains of APL and Sea-Land set the pattern for early doublestack operations. Soon thereafter, other ocean carriers, including Maersk, NYK, K-Line, and others, started dedicated doublestack trains from the West Coast. The introduction of "common-user" service by BN in 1986 led to far greater flexibility in doublestack operations. Today, the actual number of doublestack trains departing in a given week will vary considerably, depending on:

- – Weekly fluctuations in container traffic;

- – The extent to which low-volume trains are combined;

- – The volume of overflow traffic; and

- – The portion of non-dedicated intermodal trains made up of doublestack cars.

The number of cars and containers on a train will also vary widely from week to week. Significantly, almost none of the doublestack trains operating in late 1988 were true unit trains in the sense of having a fixed car consist.

1988 Railroad Doublestack Operations

At the end of 1988, there were over 100 regularly scheduled doublestack trains operated by US railroads. All of the largest railroads were operating doublestack trains, and doublestack services were beginning to spread to regional railroads as well.

The Double-Stack Network. The US doublestack train network is shown in Figure 4-1 as of late 1988. Each of the seven major railroads – Santa Fe, Burlington Northern, Conrail, CSX, Norfolk Southern, Southern Pacific and Union Pacific – was operating numerous stack train services, including dedicated trains, common-user trains and blocks of doublestack traffic on other intermodal trains. Of the next smaller group of railroads – Soo Line, Chicago & North Western, Grand Trunk Western,

Delaware & Hudson/New York, Susquehanna & Western, and Iowa Interstate, – all offered some doublestack service. Kansas City Southern, Illinois Central, and the remaining portions of the Guilford System (Boston & Maine, Maine Central) did not participate in doublestack movements as of late 1988. IC formerly provided a St. Louis-Chicago link for some SP doublestacks that have since switched to BN or Soo routes.

Other than the Iowa Interstate and the NYS&W, none of the new regional carriers provided regular doublestack service. These regional railroads were formed from trackage sold by the Class I carriers, which is unlikely to include major intermodal corridors or hubs.

Atchison, Topeka and Santa Fe. The Atchison. Topeka and Santa Fe Railroad (ATSF, or Santa Fe) had some initialdoubts about the long-term durability of the equipment and the viability of doublestack trains, especially regarding the inability of stack cars to carry other types of traffic and the apparent surrender of westbound marketing to the steamship lines. As doublestack services and marketing practices matured, however, Santa Fe and other railroads found ways to cope with those drawbacks (Figure 4-2).

In early 1989, Santa Fe was operating a dedicated weekly Los Angeles-Chicago doublestack train, for Hyundai. A portion of the Hyundai train continued to New York via Conrail. ATSF also offered several daily common user intermodal departures from Los Angeles which could carry doublestacked containers. ATSF's major traffic lanes were Los Angeles-Chicago and Los Angeles Houston/Dallas, with service offered to all major intermediate points, notably Kansas City. ATSF also operated a Los Angeles-Memphis intermodal service in conjunction

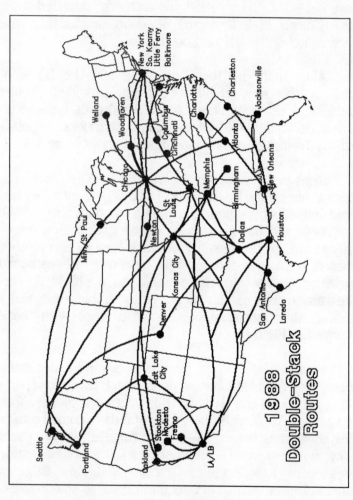

Figure 4-1

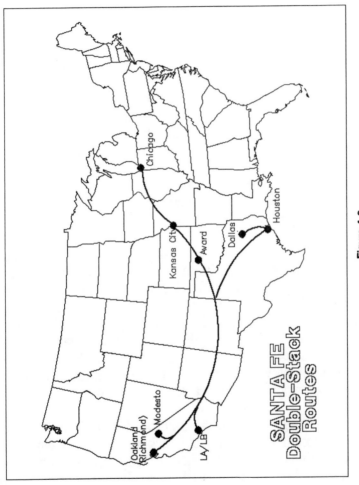

Figure 4-2

with BN. Mitsui O.S.K. Lines was a major user of the ATSF common-user intermodal operations.

From Northern California, ATSF operated a weekly dedicated train for Maersk originating in Richmond. This train operated through Santa Fe's Franklin Canyon and Tehachapi tunnels, and so was limited to two 8-foot 6-inch high containers on each platform. ATSF also operated three or more daily intermodal trains to and from Richmond that handled marine containers.

Santa Fe also provided a domestic container service in conjunction with the Modesto and Empire Traction, probably the shortest shortline handling stack cars. The service originated at the Valley Lift facility at Modesto, Calif., and the containers moved primarily to Chicago and Kansas City. Wineries were a major traffic source, but the service also handled other agricultural products from the San Joaquin Valley.

ATSF's common-user trains were operated under the "EconoStack" program, which was started in April 1986. To support EconoStack operations and its dedicated trains, ATSF set up neutral chassis pools in Chicago (operated by XTRA) and Los Angeles (operated by Flexi-Van). In July 1988, ATSF inaugurated "Quality Stack" service between Los Angeles and New York under an arrangement with Conrail that gave Santa Fe control of service, pricing and marketing.

Burlington Northern. BN can be credited with the first "common-user" doublestack services. Six-day-per – week trains were established in 1985 to serve steamship lines at the Ports of Seattle and Tacoma. The Port of Seattle, which had shippers agent authority, was considering operation of port-controlled trains, and BN created its own common-user service as an alternative. Under this arrangement, ocean carriers commited to an annual volume at a favorable rate, rather than contracting for a dedicated train.

At the start of 1989, BN was operating both dedicated and common-user doublestack trains to and from the Pacific Northwest ports (Figure 4-3). The dedicated doublestack trains operating on BN were Sea-Land's, which originated in Tacoma. Two Sea-Land trains operated between Tacoma and Chicago, and a third train operated between Tacoma and Little Ferry, N.J., via CSX and NYS&W. BN scheduled three daily common-user container trains from the Seattle International Gateway, six days per week. The major common-user route was Seattle-Minneapolis/St. Paul-Chicago. This train typically consisted of about 90% stack cars, the rest being conventional flatcars. The second route was Seattle-Omaha-Kansas City-Memphis-Birmingham. That train typically consisted of about 40% stack cars. The third route, in order of volume, was Seattle-Denver-Dallas-Houston, which occasionally used doublestack equipment but was primarily conventional. BN operated additional sections of any of these trains as required.

BN at that time moved a substantial portion of its export traffic on conventional flatcars because much of the export traffic originated away from the main urban hubs served by doublestack trains. The stack cars returned westbound with a mix of export, domestic, and empty containers. Eastbound, the Washington ports of Seattle and Tacoma have historically handled a larger proportion of 20-foot import containers than their California counterparts.

Mitsui O.S.K. Lines advertised an inland intermodal

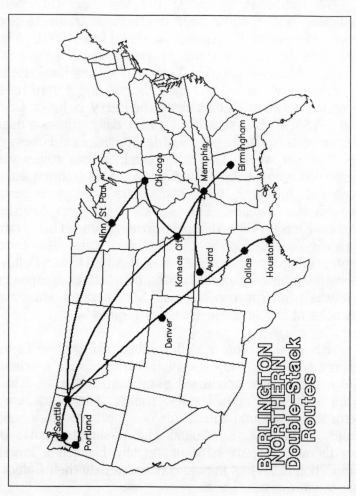

BURLINGTON
NORTHERN
Double-Stack
Routes

Figure 4-3

service that, unlike Sea-Land, APL or Maersk services, was carried on BN common-user trains eastbound. Westbound, a block of Mitsui O.S.K. Lines export traffic was separated at Spokane and operated to Portland on a BN Expediter train. From Portland the cars returned to Seattle with export or empty containers. Overflow traffic for Sea-Land and other ocean carriers was also handled on common-user trains.

BN also provided a Kansas City-Chicago connection for some SP stack trains from Southern California, and an Avard, Okla.-Memphis connection for Santa Fe.

In 1988, Burlington Northern started a domestic container service under the name "BN America," with service initially provided on the Denver-Dallas route. BN expanded domestic container service to the Seattle-Chicago and Portland-Chicago routes in early 1989, and was expected to later expand the service nationwide via agreements with connecting railroads.

Canadian National. The Canadian National Railway began weekly Vancouver-Toronto doublestack service in early 1989. The trains consisted initially of six five-platform cars each, with the equipment provided by Trailer Train. Because CN still had some clearance restrictions, the service handled only 8-foot and 8-foot 6-inch high containers, with careful matching of equipment.

Chicago and North Western. From the inception of dedicated doublestack service, Chicago and North Western has provided UP with a high speed connection between Fremont, Neb., and Chicago, where CNW developed the Global One container facility especially to handle doublestack trains (Figure 4-4). All of UP's dedicated trains for API, Maersk, and K-Line used this

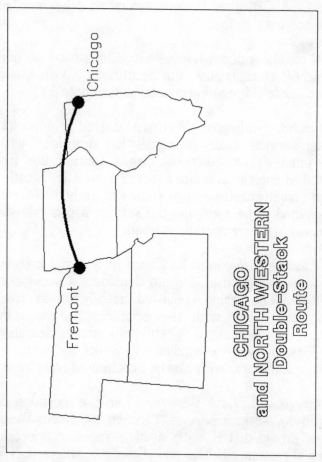

CHICAGO
and NORTH WESTERN
Double-Stack
Route

Chicago

Fremont

Figure 4-4

130

route.

As of late 1988, CNW was also providing Chicago connections for Interdom's domestic doublestack operations, and Iowa Interstate's proposed Trailer-Railer operations would also use CNW connections.

Conrail. As the early doublestack services were extended east from Chicago, Conrail became the carrier of choice for many steamship lines seeking service to and from New York. Conrail connects with the western railroads at Chicago and East St. Louis, and interchanged both entire stack trains and blocks of stack cars at both points in 1988 (Figure 4-5). Conrail operated solid trains either on its own schedules or as sections of regular intermodal trains. Blocks of doublestack cars were added to Conrail's "TrailVan" intermodal trains.

Conrail handled API's traffic between eastern intermodal hubs and the CNW interchange at Chicago. Three weekly API stack trains departed South Kearny, NJ for Chicago, where they connected with API's West Coast services via UP/CNW. Eastbound, Conrail scheduled just one complete weekly train for API between South Kearny and Los Angeles via Chicago. Conrail also, however, handled API doublestack traffic on regular TrailVans between South Kearny and Chicago six days per week.

At Chicago, Conrail also received weekly Chicago-New York Maersk and K-Line trains from CNW, and weekly NYK and MOL trains from Soo Line. These trains originated on UP and SP on the West Coast. At East St. Louis, Conrail received a block of MOL double – stack cars from SP/SSW, which carried containers destined for the Honda plant at Marysville, Ohio. The MOL

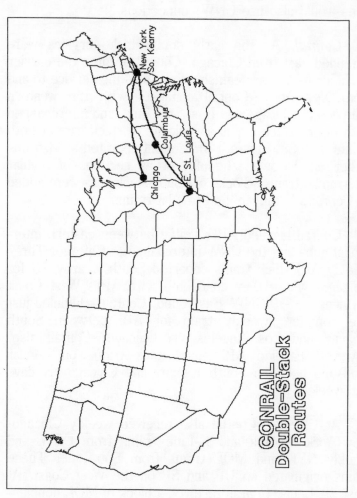

Figure 4-5

cars themselves continued on to New York, where they were combined with the Chicago-New York MOL cars for the return trip.

CSX/Sea-Land Intermodal. Since its purchase of Sea-Land, CSX has been in the unique position of operating both a railroad intermodal service and an ocean carrier that has been a major intermodal innovator. Through subsidiary CSX/Sea-Land Intermodal (CSLI), the company handled the eastern rail operations of Sea-Land trains, but cooperated with the western railroads for service in the rest of the country (Figure 4-6).

In late 1988, three trains operated weekly from SP and BN connections at Chicago to CSLI's terminal at Little Ferry, N.J.. CSLI actually operated the trains between Chicago and Buffalo, where they were interchanged with the Delaware & Hudson. The D&H, then under directed operation by the NYS&W, moved the trains to Binghamton, NY, where they were interchanged with the NYS&W proper for the last leg into Little Ferry. CSX acquired the Little Ferry terminal from the NYS&W in 1988. CSLI also operated four other routes for Sea-Land: Chicago-Atlanta (two trains per week); Chicago-Port Covington (Baltimore); New Orleans-Charleston (as part of CSX's daily Gulfwind); and New Orleans-Jacksonville.

CSLI also carried a weekly block of NYK traffic between East St. Louis and Cincinnati, and offered a Chicago-Baltimore service, originally begun by the Chessie System under an arrangement with the State of Maryland.

CSLI preferred to add stack cars to existing "doublestackable" intermodal trains wherever possible

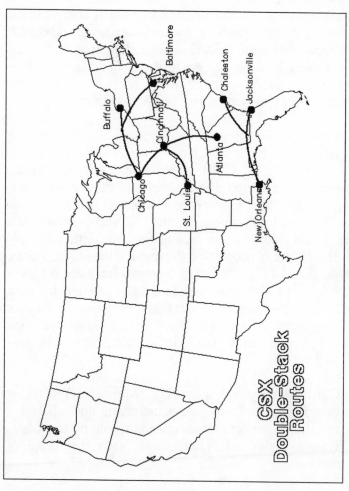

CSX
Double-Stack
Routes

Buffalo
Baltimore
Cincinnati
Chaleston
Jacksonville
Atlanta
Chicago
St. Louis
New Orleans

Figure 4-6

rather than starting new trains. One example was the Gulfwind, which took the place of both the former United States Lines stack train between Savannah and New Orleans, and the former Evergreen stack train from Charleston.

Through its CSX Distribution Services subsidiary, CSX operated neutral chassis pools and container maintenance facilities in Jacksonville, Nashville and New Orleans. CSX expected to establish similar operations in Chicago, Atlanta and Memphis.

Florida East Coast. The Florida East Coast Railroad was providing conventional service between Jacksonville and Miami for CSLI traffic in late 1988.

Grand Trunk Western. As of late 1988, Grand Trunk Western (GTW) was handling API doublestack traffic between Chicago and Detroit (Figure 4-7). The API traffic was originally handled at GTW's intermodal facility, but API opened its own facility at Woodhaven, 18 miles from Detroit on GTW property. GTW was also providing daily stack car connections with BN and Santa Fe to serve Detroit and Flat Rock. GTW planned to extend service to Battle Creek in 1989.

Iowa Interstate. Iowa Interstate (IAIS), a short regional railroad, operated a unique domestic doublestack service for Interdom, Inc., using a fleet of leased doublestack cars and containers (including 150 48-foot-long, 102-inch-wide containers built especially for domestic service). Interdom's service was based in Newton, Iowa (near Des Moines, Figure 4-8) where Maytag Appliance has a major plant, and Maytag provided the original start-up traffic. IAIS operated from a recently upgraded intermodal facility in Newton over a combina-

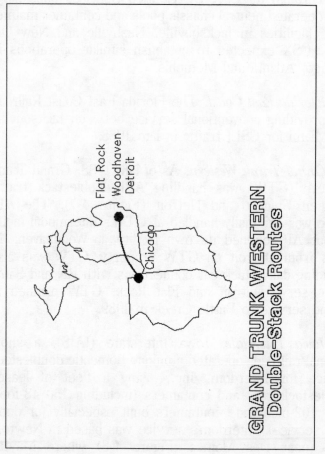

GRAND TRUNK WESTERN
Double-Stack Routes

Flat Rock
Woodhaven
Detroit

Chicago

Figure 4-7

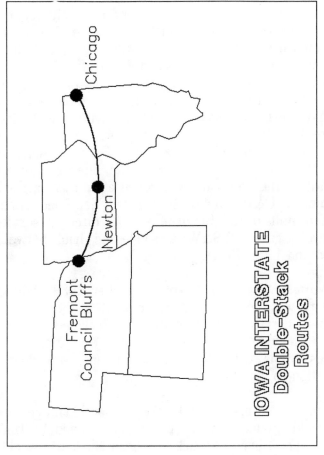

IOWA INTERSTATE
Double-Stack
Routes

Figure 4-8

tion of its own lines and trackage rights between Blue Island, Ill. and Council Bluffs, Iowa, providing daily service in the Chicago-Los Angeles corridor in conjunction with UP and CNW. IAIS and Interdom were moving roughly 200 loads per week in late 1988.

New York, Susquehanna & Western. The Susquehanna (NYS&W) was for several years the only regional railroad involved in doublestack traffic. Sea-Landtrains between Binghamton, N.Y. and Little Ferry, N.J. have made up a large part of NYS&W's traffic base, and NYS&W reporting marks appear on many of Sea-Land's doublestack cars. The trains use a combination of NYS&W's own trackage and trackage rights over Conrail (Figure 4-9). In 1988, that operation was changed in two ways. First NYS&W sold the Little Ferry terminal to CSLI. Second, NYS&W became the directed service operator of the Delaware & Hudson after that carrier's bankruptcy. D&H previously handled Sea-Land trains between Buffalo and Binghamton; the directed service effectively gave NYS&W a single-line haul between Buffalo and Little Ferry.

Norfolk Southern. As of December 1988, Norfolk Southern was moving API's traffic south of the Chicago-New York corridor (Figure 4-10). This included Chicago-Atlanta service. NS also interchanged Atlanta-Los Angeles trains with SP at New Orleans, providing a connection to Charlotte.

For K-Line and Maersk, Norfolk Southern operated two weekly round trips between Chicago and Welland, Ontario. For Hanjin, Norfolk Southern handled a weekly movement between BN at Chicago and NYS&W at Buffalo destined for Secaucus, N.J.. Maersk was expected to add service between Chicago and Montreal, with

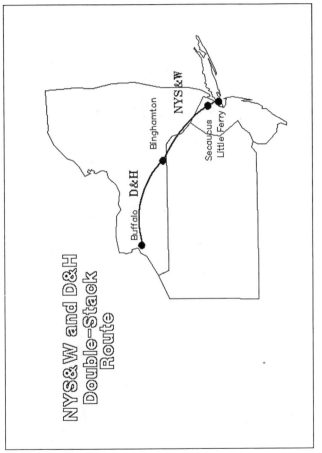

Figure 4-9

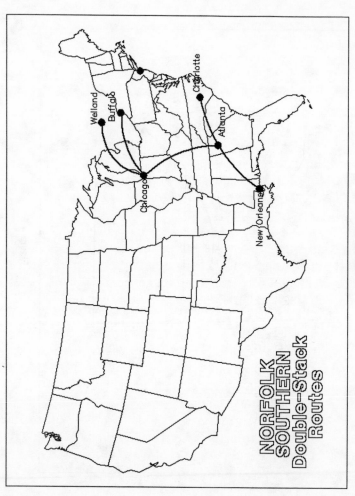

NORFOLK
SOUTHERN
Double-Stack
Routes

Welland
Buffalo
Charlotte
Atlanta
Chicago
New Orleans

Figure 4-10

140

NS to move the trains through Buffalo.

In the Buffalo-Chicago corridor, Norfolk Southern was operating some short stack trains with two-man crews. Four trains per week in each direction were operating with reduced crews. Normal train consist was one locomotive and up to nine five-platform cars (45 platforms, 90 FEU).

Soo Line. The Soo Line provided SP with a Kansas City-Chicago route for those clients not using BN (Figure 4-11).

Southern Pacific Lines. After the 1988 purchase by Rio Grande Industries, the Southern Pacific Lines (SP) included Southern Pacific, Cotton Belt (St.Louis Southwestern), and Denver & Rio Grande Western. Southern Pacific pioneered the doublestack car, putting the first into service in 1981. Those cars were built to handle SP's Sea-Land traffic and were mixed into regularly scheduled intermodal trains over SP's southern corridor route. SP began adding both dedicated trains and common user trains in 1984 and 1985.

Construction of the Los Angeles Intermodal Container Transfer Facility (ICTF) serving the Ports of Los Angeles and Long Beach gave SP a competitive advantage in the largest doublestack market. SP was quick to exploit that advantage, and the growth of container traffic through the ICTF exceeded expectations. At the same time, tunnel clearance restrictions and the uncertain future of the Central Corridor (Overland Route) in the projected SP-Santa Fe merger discouraged marketing efforts in Northern California. The result was that SP became the largest single carrier of Southern California doublestack traffic while carrying almost none to or from

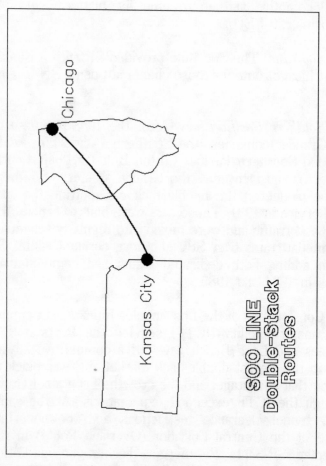

SOO LINE
Double-Stack
Routes

Chicago

Kansas City

Figure 4-11

Northern California (Figure 4-12).

SP scheduled four daily eastbound common-user doublestack train departures from the ICTF in late 1988. These trains were destined for Chicago, Memphis, Houston and interchange with Conrail at St. Louis. Three daily westbound trains to Los Angeles departed from Pine Bluff, Ark., New Orleans and a BN interchange at Kansas City. Other stack or conventional cars returned on regular SP intermodal trains. On days when traffic was light, some of the eastbound trains were combined as far as El Paso or some other intermediate point.

In late 1988, SP operated dedicated doublestack trains for several major steamship lines. Sea-Land had a daily dedicated train to Memphis, and three weekly trains: one to New Orleans on Monday, and Chicago trains on Monday and Wednesday. A daily Sea-Land train returned westbound from Memphis. Mitsui O.S.K. Lines had two dedicated departures on SP, both on Sunday. The first split to serve Chicago and St. Louis, and the second served Memphis. The Memphis train returned westbound intact, and the Chicago and St. Louis westbound blocks were combined as a single train. Three weekly dedicated trains were operated from the ICTF for Evergreen departing Saturday and Tuesday for Chicago, and Tuesday for New Orleans and Memphis. The two Chicago trains returned westbound, and the westbound Memphis and New Orleans trains were combined. SP originated two weekly trains at the ICTF for NYK: the first on Sunday to St. Louis, using SP's original ACF-built doublestack cars, and the second on Friday to serve both Chicago and St. Louis.

Express Systems Intermodal (ESI) is a domestic

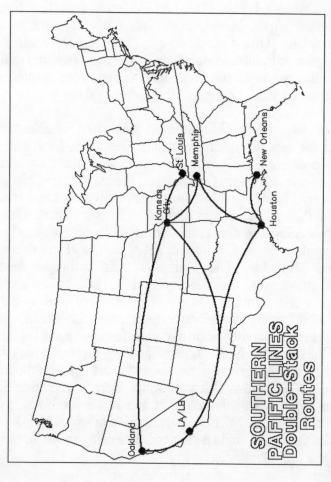

Figure 4-12

subsidiary of Orient Overseas Container Lines (OOCL). Besides arranging doublestack service for OOCL's marine containers, ESI solicited container traffic for other steamship lines and third parties. SP scheduled 13 weekly departures for ESI, six of which were dedicated trains. The six dedicated trains departed the ICTF on Sunday for Memphis, Monday for Houston and Chicago, Wednesday for Chicago, Thursday for Houston, and Saturday for Chicago. All these trains had westbound counterparts. A daily scheduled service for Memphis typically operated as part of another SP train.

Despite API's use of Union Pacific on other western routes, SP originated six weekly trains on the Southern Corridor for American President Intermodal. Three operated on Sunday, Wednesday and Friday via Houston to Atlanta via interchange with Norfolk Southern at New Orleans. The other three operated Saturday, Tuesday and Thursday to Memphis via Dallas. The westbound Memphis and New Orleans trains were combined.

SP thus scheduled over 50 weekly doublestack departures from the ICTF in late 1988. The actual number of trains in a given week depended on which scheduled departures were combined as a single train, and whether overflow traffic required extra trains for some schedules. While the dedicated trains operated for steamship companies generally consisted of only stack cars, the SP common-user trains also carried containers or trailers on conventional cars as required.

At the end of 1988, SP began offering common-user doublestack service to and from Oakland via the Central Corridor over the Sierra Nevada. Previously, stack cars sometimes operated to or from Oakland as extensions of Southern Corridor trains. Starting in December 1988, stack cars were handled eastbound on the daily Oakland-Memphis train and westbound on the Pine Bluff-Oakland train. By using both sides of its double-track Roseville-Sparks main-line to avoid the tightest tunnels and snowsheds, SP found it could accommodate combinations of 8-foot 6-inch and 9-foot 6-inch containers on stack trains until tunnel clearance improvements would permit stacked high-cube boxes.

Union Pacific. In late 1983, Union Pacific cooperated with American President Lines to run the first experimental train of doublestack cars between Los Angeles and Chicago. Dedicated UP doublestack service for APL started the following year. In 1988, all doublestack trains on Union Pacific were still dedicated trains, with the major customer being API. UP's routes are shown in Figure 4-13.

UP operated seven weekly API trains from Los Angeles, six terminated in Chicago and one went on to South Kearny via Conrail. UP originated three weekly API trains to Chicago from Oakland that made pickups at Stockton and Sacramento. Connecting services (not full trains) were operated from Fresno. UP originated three weekly API trains to Chicago in Seattle. Altogether there were 13 API departures from the West Coast on UP in late 1988.

UP's westbound service for API originated at CNW's Global One doublestack facility in Chicago. These seven weekly multi-destination trains served different combinations of western hub cities. There were also three short-distance API trains carrying westbound containers from Salt Lake City to Los Angeles on UP. Many of these "trains" were in fact blocks of API traffic on regular UP intermodal schedules. Four weekly dedicated API trains

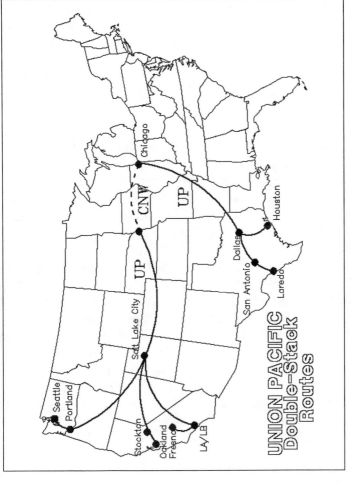

UNION PACIFIC
Double-Stack
Routes

Figure 4-13

moved from Chicago directly to Los Angeles via CNW and UP.

Another major steamship line using UP was K-Line, which had a weekly UP stack train departing from the International Transportation Services (ITS) container terminal at the Port of Long Beach. This train continued beyond the UP system to Chicago and New York via CNW and Conrail. A second weekly K-Line train operated from Tacoma to Chicago on UP and returned westbound through Portland. The last dedicated UP stack train was operated for Maersk, departing Tacoma weekly for Chicago and return.

The first stack train services expressly designed for domestic containers started in December 1988, when UP began a Chicago-Texas service in partnership with API. This doublestack train replaced a UP RoadRailer® service. From Chicago, API and UP served Dallas, Houston, San Antonio and Laredo.

UP was not offering common-user doublestack services on the BN or SP pattern, preferring to contract with steamship lines for round-trip dedicated movements. UP's daily intermodal trains from Los Angeles, Oakland, and Seattle, however, could carry containers on conventional equipment. Moreover, API solicited traffic from other ocean carriers and third parties for its stack trains operating over UP, and K-Line's purchase of a major domestic third-party shipper was expected to bring that steamship line into the domestic market as well.

Carless Services

Of the carless technologies, only the RoadRailer®

148

had entered commercial service by late 1989. In the early 1980s, most major railroads tested RoadRailers®, sometimes only for a single trip, sometimes for an extended period.

Demonstrations. In 1981, Illinois Central Gulf began regular service between Memphis and Louisville using a fleet of 80 Mark IV RoadRailers®. This service lasted about a year before discontinuance. Although the service was an operational success, it is generally conceded that traffic in that lane could not support RoadRailer® service in the long term. ICG later sold the Memphis-Louisville segment and at that time publicly questioned the commercial feasibility of intermodal service on any part of its system.

Inter-Rail Express Corp. (IREX) ran a test train of RoadRailers® into New York's Penn Station via the Hudson River tunnel in August 1982. IREX's goal was to bring shipments of Florida produce into the Hunts Point produce district using a fleet of refrigerated RoadRailers®. Production of refrigerated RoadRailers® was projected to begin in January 1983, and the IREX service was to have started in March of the same year. No fleet of refrigerated RoadRailers® was ever produced, and the service was never implemented.

The next effort at a regular RoadRailer® service was begun in November, 1982, by an operating subsidiary of Bi-Modal Corp. itself. The service, named the Empire State Xpress, served Rochester, Buffalo and New York City via Conrail. The service continued until July 1984, when it was determined that it would not reach commercial viability within the capital resources Bi-Modal had available. Reasons cited for this decision include intense competition from Buffalo to New York (by rail it is approximately 425 miles, by highway only about 375), and the inability of Bi-Modal or Conrail to secure reduced crew agreements.

The use of new technology often raises difficult institutional issues, and these issues no doubt hindered the faster adoption of RoadRailers® and other carless technologies. The potential problems surfaced dramatically in May 1986, when the operation of a RoadRailer® demonstration between Chicago and Los Angeles precipitated a short strike on Santa Fe.

Burlington Northern. In January 1986, BN instituted Chicago – St. Louis RoadRailer® service (with a highway connection to Kansas City) for interplant movements of General Motors auto parts. For this service, BN purchased the existing fleet of 220 45-foot Mark IV dry van RoadRailers®. The service continued for several months, but was withdrawn inside of a year.

Triple Crown. NS began RoadRailer® service under a separate internal organization, Triple Crown, in July 1986. The service started with the fleet of 220 45-foot Mark IV units leased from BN, and a similar number of 48-foot Mark IV RoadRailers® purchased by Norfolk Southern. Like the BN service, Triple Crown service was begun with a base traffic of auto parts between Detroit and Atlanta. Triple Crown service has grown to serve other commodities (notably paper products and foodstuffs) and other points (including Chicago, St Louis, Fort Wayne, Alexandria, VA and Jacksonville). As shown in Figure 4-14, the pattern of service in late 1988 was an abbreviated hub and spoke, with the hub being Fort Wayne. In its first full year of operation, 1987, Triple Crown handled roughly 29,000 RoadRailer® shipments. In 1988, that number grew to about 52,000. The Triple

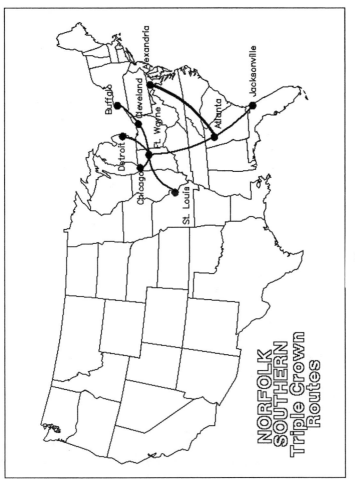

Figure 4-14

Crown RoadRailer® fleet had grown to over 1,000 units in 1988, and reached 1,750 units in 1989. The most recent additions have been Mark V units, with the demountable bogies supplied by Trailer Train.

Contrary to prevailing practice in the intermodal field, Triple Crown began as a retail operation. Although third party business has grown, the high commitment to customer service and intensive management involvement remains. These may be the keys to Triple Crowns's success to date, since the more expensive RoadRailer® equipment depends on careful management and marketing to achieve a high level of utilization and rapid turnaround.

CSX. CSX started its Xpress Railer service between Detroit and Atlanta in April 1987, again with a base traffic of auto parts. CSX no doubt drew on the experience gained on the earlier extended RoadRailer® demonstration on the Richmond, Fredricksburg and Potomac. In 1988, Xpress Railer service was being extended to Dayton, Ohio. (Figure 4-15) CSX began Xpress Railer service with 250 Mark IV RoadRailers®, and was expending that fleet by another 240 units in 1989.

Union Pacific. UP began a service using Mark V RoadRailers® between Chicago and Dallas, with highway connections to Detroit on the north and other Texas points on the south. This service too began with auto parts. UP's service began in early 1988, but was withdrawn in December 1988 in favor of a Detroit-Dallas domestic doublestack train operated by UP for American President Intermodal.

No national network of RoadRailer® services has yet

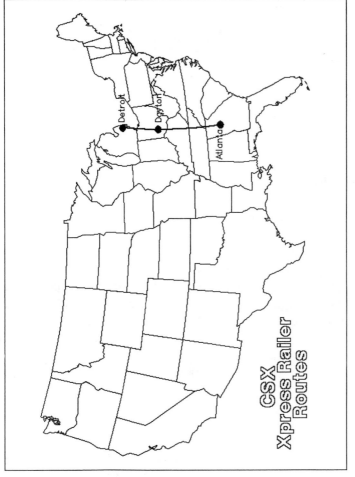

Figure 4-15

153

emerged. An ambitious proposal to form such a network was announced by Mark VII Transportation in August 1987. Mark VII envisioned a hub-and-spoke network, with services wholesaled to agents and forwarders. Mark VII had problems soliciting railroad participation, and successful implementation may remain illusive.

Although RoadRailer® services have had false starts, the commitment of Norfolk Southern and CSX to their Triple Crown and Xpress Railer initiatives indicates that RoadRailers® will finally have a fair chance to prove their market potential. Should either or both of those services prove an enduring success, they will likely expand and encourage other carriers to follow suit.

Expedited Piggyback Services

Experiments In Short-haul TOFC

Regular piggyback (TOFC) services have been available for three decades. But for most of that time, a piggyback train was not much different from any other manifest freight train. Although piggyback trains typically received the higher over-the-line priority also awarded to perishables, auto parts and other high-rated, time-sensitive business, the basis for operation – train length, crew size, service frequency – was the same for intermodal as for carload freight.

For piggyback service, the intermodal revolution started in Florida, in the early 1960s, when the management of the Florida East Coast responded to a labor strike by operating cabooseless trains with two-person crews. FEC persisted, survived the strike, and prospered under this operating system while compiling an enviable safety record. Moreover, FEC built a thriving piggyback business in the 366-mile Jacksonville-Miami corridor, which is much shorter than the 500-mile minimum often cited for competitive TOFC service. By 1978, FEC was running seven daily cabooseless piggyback trains south from Jacksonville, and taking traffic off the parallel highways.

The Illinois Central Gulf (now the Illinois Central) took the next step in 1975, when it began its "Slingshot" service between St. Louis and Chicago. The initial runs were experimental, using a two-person crew and a single locomotive to pull up to 15 cars without a caboose. The success of these initial runs encouraged ICG to negotiate with the unions for regular service on the same basis. By 1980, there were three daily Slingshot trains each way, each covering the 280-mile haul in eight hours. ICG found that even with "productivity pay" compensation for the reduced crew size, the lower overall labor costs justified substantial rate cuts to attract traffic. Although ICG's Slingshot trains were ultimately discontinued, they attracted the interest of other railroads and led to more successful and enduring services.

The Federal Railroad Administration sponsored a similar experiment on the Milwaukee Road beginning in 1978. With FRA's financial support, the Milwaukee started operating piggyback "Sprint" trains between Minneapolis/St. Paul and Chicago. Labor agreements provided for three three-person crews to cover the 400-mile run, rather than the four-person crews as required on other freight trains. The cabooseless Sprints were limited to 25 cars and 60 mph, and with a 10-hour one-way schedule could make one daily round trip. By late 1978. Sprint service was up to 42 trains per week. The following year the service reached profitability, and could be weaned from FRA's support. New owner Soo Line has maintained Sprint service after buying the Milwaukee.

These three railroads pioneering expedited TOFC services had five things in common:

1. Reduced crews

2. No caboose

3. Short lengths of haul

4. Limited train length

5. Fast, frequent service

The crew size reductions and cabooseless operations were negotiated with the unions (except, of course, on the FEC) based on limited train length, the lack of intermediate switching, and – above all – the promise of new rail traffic diverted from trucks and the long-term jobs thus created. All three services sought to attract traffic in corridors where there was little or no existing TOFC traffic to cannibalize, so new traffic had to – and did – come from the highways. The service frequency is the flip side of the train length: if the railroads had held the trains to accumulate 50 or 100 piggyback cars, the delay would have ended any hopes of competing with trucks. While daily dedicated TOFC trains are the norm in most long-haul corridors, many successful short-haul services feature multiple daily departures.

Leading-edge Piggyback Services

At least four railroads have since adopted these

principles to create short-haul, truck-competitive piggy-back services. From quasi-experimental starts in just a few corridors, these services have spread to form the leading edge of piggyback operations and marketing.

Santa Fe's Quality Service Network In 1987, coming off the disappointment of the rejected merger with SP, Santa Fe launched its Quality Service Network (QSN) of short, fast TOFC trains. Over the next two years, and with union cooperation, Santa Fe expanded QSN opera-tions to most of the corridors where there was a fighting chance of capturing truck traffic. And the QSN trains did indeed capture truck traffic, as Santa Fe saw the return of traffic that had long since been written off as gone for good. Moreover, the QSN trains have attracted their own business without eroding Santa Fe's strong longhaul trailer traffic base. As Figure 4-16 shows, by 1989 the Quality Service Network included some 15 city pairs, each receiving frequent service with short, cabooseless trains manned by reduced crews operating over longer distances between crew changes.

BN's Expediters. As part of its intermodal expansion in the 1980s, Burlington Northern established "Expedi-ter" trains to challenge trucks over the shorter hauls. Cabooseless, limited to 60 cars, and running with reduced crews, these trains were intended to generate new business rather than to cannibalize BN's existing TOFC traffic. As Figure 4-17 shows, the Expediter network covers much of the former St. Louis-San Fran-cisco (Frisco) territory BN acquired by merger in 1980. Two routes stand out. One is the Chicago-Detroit connec-tion provided under BN's 1984 Voluntary Coordination Agreement with Grand Trunk Western. The second is the Portland-Seattle segment, which appears from Figure 4-17 to be isolated, but actually interconnects with BN's

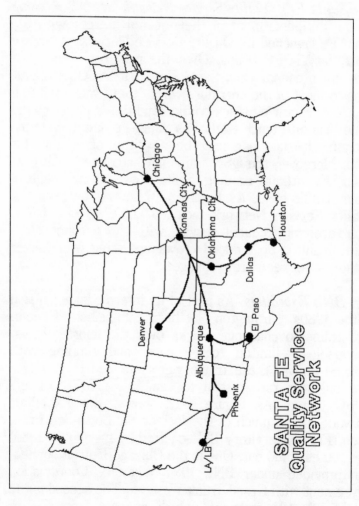

SANTA FE
Quality Service
Network

Figure 4-16

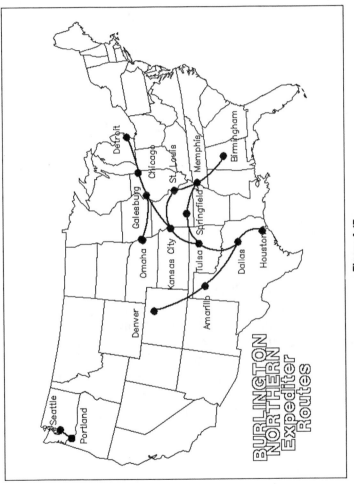

BURLINGTON NORTHERN Expediter Routes

Seattle
Portland
Detroit
Chicago
St. Louis
Memphis
Birmingham
Galesburg
Springfield
Omaha
Kansas City
Tulsa
Dallas
Houston
Denver
Amarillo

Figure 4-17

159

non-Expediter intermodal services (including domestic doublestacks under the BN America banner).

SP/DRGW's Track Stars and Rail Blazers. What became SP's "Track Star" program began in 1983, with the "Texas Overnight Piggyback Express" between Houston and Dallas. The SP trains were limited to 15 cars and one locomotive, and in common with other services had a two-person crew and no caboose. One such crew covered the entire 263-mile route. Initial success in attracting traffic from the highways led SP to start a Phoenix-Los Angeles train (the "Sun Pig," with two-person crews) and two "West Coast Track Stars," Oakland-Portland and Los Angeles-Portland (with three–person crews). By 1987, SP added El Paso-Kansas City-St. Louis service (the "Rio Grande Star") and Dallas-Pine Bluff-St. Louis/Memphis service (the "Cotton Belt Track Stars"). After the 1988 merger with Rio Grande, SP added Houston-Dallas-El Paso – Phoenix service (the "Lone Star"), Kansas City-Denver service (the "Kansas City Star"), and connecting service to the San Joaquin Valley of California (the "San Joaquin Star"). New Track Stars also provide service between Houston and New Orleans, and Houston and Eagle Pass via San Antonio. The merger brought DRGW's Denver-Salt Lake City "RailBlazers" into the system. As the 80's drew to a close, SP was planning to add Oakland-Salt Lake City service, bringing expedited, reduced-crew piggyback service to the entire Southern Pacific System (Figure 4-18). A key feature of SP's effort is intensive marketing to promote the new trains.

CNGT's Lasers. The "Laser" trains operated jointly by Canadian National and its subsidiary Grand Trunk Western are unique in several ways. Since 1985, these trains have used specially designed well-type articulated

160

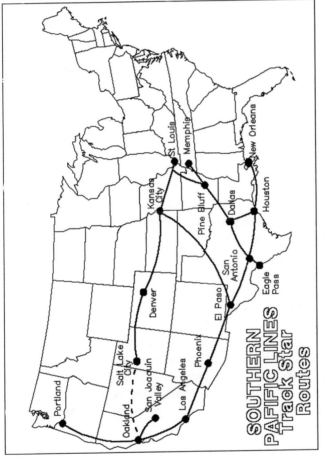

Figure 4-18

SOUTHERN
PAFIFIC LINES
Track Star
Routes

St Louis
Memphis
New Orleans
Kansas City
Pine Bluff
Dallas
Houston
San Antonio
Eagle Pass
Denver
El Paso
Phoenix
Salt Lake City
San Joaquin Valley
Los Angeles
Oakland
Portland

cars, similar to IBC doublestack cars, to bring piggyback trailers and containers with or without chassis through the 19th century clearances of the Port Huron tunnel. Over Grand Trunk from Chicago and through the tunnel, Lasers operate with reduced crews and without cabooses. At Sarnia, on the Canadian end of the tunnel, a caboose is added and a full crew takes over to forward the trains to Montreal and as far as Moncton, New Brunswick (Figure 4-19). Although limited to 60 platforms, on the CN the Lasers are otherwise much like other intermodal trains. Daily service has been offered since 1985, and steady traffic growth justified the start of twice-daily service in 1989.

A New Standard

At the threshold of the 1990s, the Sprints, QSNs, Expediters, Track Stars and Lasers have ceased to be experiments. They now represent an emerging standard for the piggyback service and marketing required for the highly competitive movements under 500 miles. Crew size reductions and cabooseless operations hold down costs, while short, frequent trains maintain the necessary service quality.

The labor cost reductions that keep these trains competitive were accepted by the unions with the expectation that these trains could add new traffic, and in the long run, new jobs, and they have. Each of these leading-edge services must be a joint effort, for the responsibility of attracting and holding that new traffic rests on railroad marketers as well as on the operating personnel.

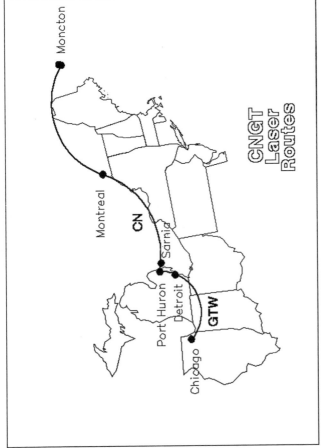

Figure 4-19

163

Chapter 5

INTERMODAL INFRASTRUCTURE

Ports

The growth of intermodal transportation has had a profound effect on the port industry in North America. As the Shipping Act of 1984 began to change the way carriers viewed their business, port directors responded by developing marketing strategies designed to attract major steamship carriers to their intermodal facilities. The doublestack train was the first innovation to prompt a rethinking among port managers, and it led to a major change in marine transportation policy, namely decisions by major steamship carriers to build marine vessels too large to pass through the Panama Canal. Thus, the June 6, 1988, arrival at the Port of Los Angeles of the President Truman, the first of American President Lines' new C10 vessels, was more than just a ceremony. It signified the beginning of a new era of port and marine terminal management. It also cemented the initial commitment to modern intermodal transportation made when stack trains first came into operation.

The marine carrier market itself has become a major factor in port planning. Statistics for the US port business indicate that 74% of total container traffic flows through the ten largest ports and that ten carriers handle over 70% of containers in these ports. This places carriers at an even greater competitive advantage vis-a-vis ports, since no port can afford to lose one of its major accounts.

Port competition has also begun to blur distinctions

Figure 5-1 The S.S. *President Truman*, one of American President Companies new wide-bodied C10-class vessels, can carry 4,300 20-foot equivalent units of cargo. Courtesy American President Companies.

between traditional transportation roles. Several ports, for example, have attempted to establish their own transportation projects, much to the chagrin of their customers in some instances. As early as 1984, only months after APL's inaugural doublestack train service, the Port of Seattle announced its intention to begin its own doublestack service to Chicago and the East Coast, raising questions about the propriety of an entity funded in part by public money entering private business. The Ports of Los Angeles and Long Beach also considered sponsoring their own trains until finally abandoning the idea in 1989.

On the West Coast, where the impact of stack trains was first felt, individual ports have steadily increased their marketing efforts in an attempt to influence the routing of imported containerized shipments moving from the Far East to major Midwest and East Coast markets. The sheer volume of eastbound traffic has resulted in intense competition between West Coast ports, both within and among the three major port regions.

A similar effect has been felt in other areas, although for slightly different reasons. For example, the rivalry between the Port of Baltimore and those of the Virginia Ports Authority for export traffic flowing from the Midwest by rail and for import traffic from the Atlantic Ocean provides a good example of the growing competition among East Coast ports. This competition has spawned the Virginia Inland Port and the Sea Girt terminal – both innovative and aggressive developments in the increasingly sophisticated intermodal arena. The race to develop an efficient "land-water interface" has also been characterized by increased competition in most areas. In this respect technological development has become a major preoccupation of port planners and

Figure 5-2 Unloading operations of a Maersk container ship at the Port of Oaklands Outer Harbor typify the high level of container activity at West Coast ports. Courtesy Port of Oakland

terminal designers. Most of them focus their attention in one area: the development of an intermodal container transfer facility and the equipment to be used in it.

Intermodal Container Transfer Facilities

The "doublestack revolution" in intermodal container traffic has been widely proclaimed. Whether or not it is a true revolution, it has focused attention on the tremendous growth in ocean-to-rail intermodal traffic, and presented ports with a new and vital planning issue. Ports compete vigorously for discretionary intermodal cargo and, as intermodal volumes have increased, the costs and delays in ocean-to-rail container transfer have come under closer scrutiny. In the past, port planning ended at the marine terminal gate; today it extends to the rail container transfer facility.

Ports throughout the US, and particularly those on the West Coast, are taking a hard look at ways to improve the ocean-to-rail transfer, with "on-dock" facilities being the leading choice in many cases. Yet on-dock facilities are not panaceas, and their development raises a number of serious operational and organizational issues. Domestic container traffic is one potential stumbling block, and railroad access is another.

Even if a port area facility could be devoted exclusively to maritime traffic, the complexity of that traffic alone may force planners away from single-purpose designs, and force them to dedicate precious acreage to the storage areas and buffer zones needed to cope with that complexity. Recognizing that some domestic container traffic will be inevitably mixed with maritime traffic, at least for the foreseeable future, provisions must be made to handle such traffic without unnecessary disruption to the maritime flow. While a simplified view of ocean-rail intermodal transfer connects one inbound ship with one doublestack unit train, in reality the relationship is more complex, and the port development alternatives must accommodate that complexity.

Containers from a single large ocean carrier such as APL or Sea-Land will be split among these categories for subsequent movement by rail:

– Ocean carrier traffic to or from major hubs via dedicated doublestack trains.

– Ocean carrier traffic to or from major or secondary hubs via common-user or regular intermodal trains, including overflow from dedicated trains.

– Third-party traffic to major hubs or secondary points moving on common-user regular intermodal trains (with or without chassis).

The rail facility handling of these three categories may be radically different. For example, the rail carrier might not consider the third category to be "maritime" traffic at all, since the rail customer is a shipper or third party. And to the extent that containers are returned empty, yet another category needs to be considered.

Whereas the engineering questions involved in the design of new facilities have certainly been interesting, they have paled in comparison with the political disputes and market posturing ports have indulged in concerning their use. The debate, for example, over whether "on-dock" or "off-dock" rail transfer development makes most sense has become a major marketing issue.

Current facilities range from "on-dock" transfers in or adjacent to the marine terminal, to separate rail facilities 20 miles or more away. The choice of one arrangement over another depends less on the issue of distance than on issues of jurisdiction and transfer cost. In the off-dock scenario the container typically passes from the ocean carrier's jurisdiction to a drayman at the marine terminal gate, and from the drayman to the railroad at the rail yard gate. Two inspections are performed in this procedure, with two sets of documents and attendant delays. Since the drayage cost is based on time, the ocean carrier sees delay as a direct cost. One alternative to the double-transfer system is to eliminate drayage by bringing the rail transfer "on-dock." In such a system, the container passes directly from the ocean carrier to the railroad, with only one inspection and only one set of paperwork.

Other things being equal, the ability to provide on-dock intermodal transfer and eliminate drayage appears to be a competitive advantage for discretionary cargo. Things are seldom equal, however, and savings in drayage may be offset by gate fees or terminal productivity differences. On-dock transfers now take place in Tacoma, Portland, San Francisco and Long Beach. The ports of Seattle and Oakland are in the process of adding on-dock rail transfer at some terminals. Ports and railroads that do not offer on-dock transfer have felt compelled to pursue other strategies to remain competitive.

Nevertheless the "on-dock" controversy is far from resolved. As with so many emerging issues, a discussion of the issues must begin with definitions and clarifications. In this case, the subject is transfer of ocean-going

ISO containers between ships and railcars. Where and how that might best take place is a subject of vigorous debate among ocean carriers, ports and railroads.

The premise of on-dock transfer is that the transfer should take place within the confines of the marine terminal, rather than draying the container over public roads to another facility. As it happens, this simple premise becomes complex if we examine the numerous ways in which it can be implemented. The issues to be faced in implementing on-dock transfer go to the heart of intermodalism itself: reconciling the incentives and characteristics of the participants to realize the full potential of intermodal transportation.

On-dock transfer is not as ambitious or demanding as direct transfer between ship and rail. Some European terminals can load railcars at shipside, using the container crane to move containers to or from the ship without an intermediate vehicle or point of rest. Many North American marine terminals have railroad tracks within reach of the container cranes for transfer of non-standard cargo, so direct ship-to-rail container transfer is possible and has probably been done from time to time. But no North American port has maintained a direct ship-to-rail transfer of significant volume or duration, and none do so now. The on-dock transfer systems in North America use either a vehicle or ground storage as an intermediary between the ship and the railroad cars.

In North America, then, "on-dock" usually means "inside the marine terminal," and the boundary is defined by the entry and exit gates, where the formalities of interchange, inspection and paperwork take place. Most on-dock transfers are separated from the ship by at least the width of the marine terminal, and do not correspond at all to the mental image of direct shipside transfer.

In other words, it is function that defines on-dock transfer, not proximity to the ship. The objective of on-dock transfer is to reduce the cost, time and administrative effort required to shift containers between the ship and the railroad.

On-dock terminals are the norm at major Canadian ports. Halifax (Halterm), Vancouver (Vanterm), and Saint John (Brunterm) all have rail transfer facilities within large, multi-user marine terminals. While US ports may agonize over the difficulties of adding on-dock transfers to existing marine terminals, the Canadian terminals were designed to include rail transfer from the beginning. But they have yet to handle doublestack trains on a regular basis.

An important feature of the major Canadian on-dock rail transfers is that they serve large, multi-user marine terminals. Terminals on this scale can, if properly designed, accommodate an efficiently sized rail transfer in a configuration that reduces or eliminates interference with container yard activity. It is difficult to add on-dock rail transfer to existing marine terminals, especially single-user terminals which may not have sufficient overall length.

The development of on-dock transfer on the US West Coast has proceeded quite differently than in Canada. The ports of the Pacific Northwest, Northern California, and Southern California serve the burgeoning transpacific trade, and originate a fleet of eastbound doublestack trains. Under pressure to handle those trains efficiently, and in tight competition with one another, US West Coast ports have turned to on-dock transfer as a

173

selling point. Ports that have it advance claims for its efficiency. Ports that do not yet have on-dock transfer are studying it, or looking for other ways to provide the same benefits.

The theoretical advantages of on-dock transfer lie in the complete elimination of one or more operations from the chain of lifts and moves required between ship and rail. The dray is usually the target, but most on-dock transfers internalize the transport function of the dray rather than avoiding it.

Despite the theoretical advantages of on-dock transfer and its apparent successful implementation in Canadian and US ports, it may not be the best course of development for every port. Certainly, ports which have new off-dock facilities (such as Los Angeles/Long Beach or Seattle), or ports that would have to fit on-dock facilities into fully developed terminals (such as Oakland), may want to consider other means of obtaining the same benefits. While ports typically encourage ocean carrier and railroad arrangements from a neutral stance, they also typically bear the capital cost of on-dock transfer facilities. A recent article commented that doublestack trains were becoming to ports what television antennas were to 1950s homeowners – you have not "arrived" if you do not have one yet. Must every port provide on-dock transfer as well?

If on-dock transfer eliminates drayage, its attraction depends on which party is paying for the drayage. In most locations, the ocean carrier pays for drayage. A reduction in overall cost, however, does not necessarily mean a reduction in the charges paid by the carriers involved. The port or terminal owner needs to recover the capital costs of an on-dock facility and to do so some on-dock facilities (and new off-dock facilities, as well) assess charges on each container. If containers are drayed to railroad-operated intermodal yards, the actual transfer between chassis and railcar is included in the rail rate. Will the railroad be willing to rebate the transfer cost if it must incur switching costs at an on-dock transfer? Some railroad contract rates include drayage at the port, making the ocean carrier largely indifferent to the transfer cost. Who, then, has any incentive to pursue on-dock transfer? Moreover, small differences in inter-modal transfer costs may not signify much to railroads and ocean carriers who have traditionally equalized rates over large geographic areas.

Another factor to be considered is the fact that space is at a premium in modern container terminals, and a rail transfer facility takes up space. Worse yet, efficient rail facilities tend to be long and narrow, and do not fit well with the boxier, oblong shape of marine terminals. The problem is exacerbated by stack cars, which come in 265-foot to 290-foot units, or about one-quarter to one-third the length of a typical berth. Even a small number of such cars could seriously disrupt traffic flow in a single-user terminal. The multi-berth, multi-user marine terminal can more easily accommodate a rail facility.

Brunterm, at Saint John, New Brunswick, handles railcars in the midst of a multi-user marine terminal, enabling front-end loaders to move export containers direct to the stack. Halterm, in Halifax, has a 1,750-foot (537 meter) total berth length, permitting construction of a substantial rail facility along the back side of the terminal. Although smaller overall, Portland's Terminal 6 has a similar concept. Sea-Land and Maersk both load their Tacoma trains on-dock, in the functional sense, but neither transfer takes place within the marine terminal proper. Maersk, at Terminal 7, uses Tacoma's North Intermodal Yard, which runs between Terminals 4 and 7 and serves both. Sea-Land uses Tacoma's South Intermodal Yard, which is a small, conventional rail container yard accessible to Sea-Land's yard tractors and chassis via a short private connection beneath an elevated public road. The K-Line Long Beach train is loaded on the periphery of the ITS terminal there, again outside the working marine terminal.

The most important factor that determines the cost of moving a container between the marine terminal and the rail yard is time: time to find and mount the container, time to hook up the chassis and inspect the container, time to complete and check paperwork, and more time for delays at any point. The whole process must be reversed at the rail end. It is the gate, and the functions it symbolizes, that raises drayage prices far above the cost of merely transporting the container. At the marine terminal gate, the container passes from the jurisdiction of the ocean carrier to the jurisdiction of the drayman. At the rail yard gate, the container passes from the jurisdiction of the drayman to the jurisdiction of the railroad.

Exactly what is it that on-dock transfer avoids? First, on-dock transfer reduces two interchange processes to one simplified procedure. Second, on-dock transfer avoids the use of highway licensed and equipped drayage equipment. Third, on-dock transfer avoids highway weight limits, which prevent 40-foot containers from being loaded to their ISO weight capacities, though this attribute tends to create a problem if containers that exceed highway weight limits are moved inland from port regions to their ultimate destination.

On-dock transfer is not a technological or operational innovation, but an organizational and institutional one. The accomplishment is not bringing the railcar close to the ship, but bringing it inside the gate. There are other ways in which most or all of the benefits of on-dock transfer can be obtained: public highway easements, streamlined paperwork and administration, simplified work rules, neutral chassis pools, etc. But each of these measures requires difficult re-negotiation of existing institutional and regulatory arrangements. For one port or carrier to undertake all these efforts would be a Herculean task. The capital requirements of on-dock transfer facilities may be small in comparison.

In essence, on-dock transfer is a way of circumventing long-standing organizational and institutional inefficiencies. The key to efficient intermodalism is not the distance between ship and rail, but what takes place there.

On-dock transfer, like doublestack trains or intermodalism itself, is not a cure-all. Under existing practices, some ocean carriers and terminals are not candidates for on-dock transfer. Other situations that seem to clamor for on-dock transfer should be examined more closely to ensure that on-dock transfer will solve the problem. As with so many attractive innovations, we can expect to see on-dock transfer misapplied in some places.

The fact is that not all ports have the space or the geometry to develop on-dock transfer facilities, while for others extending rail lines through inner city areas is not practicable. Limitations such as these have not deterred the marketers, however. Every port has a proposed solution, and each solution has become the theme of numerous conference debates and seminars. The high level of debate may indicate that, despite the research and analysis backing many of the plans being put forward (and, in some cases, already under development), in fact there are few, if any, "right" answers for ports in general. Ports clearly have individual needs and approaches.

Port Capacity and Terminal Productivity

At the heart of all this appears to be a desire to design a port operation capable of responding to Wieger Koornstra's appeal: "Don't stop the box!" Maintaining "a continuous flow without any interruption" represents the port user's major logistic need, the A.C.L., Inc. president argued at a major port conference in 1988. Port authorities need to work as partners in the transportation chain, said Koornstra, and their role must be to provide a fully integrated service.

This would entail, for example, efficient management of relations between stevedoring, terminal handling, gate processing, and maintenance and repair functions, along with maximum development of technology such as electronic data interchange and automated Customs clearance systems. The major ports are more than what they used to be, he concluded, adding that "today it is an important crossroads of transportation of all sorts, not simply a harbor with ships."

But, not stopping the box and developing a more global perspective on port use have become complex tasks. Along with the usual environmental issues, landside access is becoming a central problem in the port planning process, both from a business and a community viewpoint.

Consider a hypothetical new 100-acre terminal, capable of handling 300,000 TEU per year. Even if most of the containers were 40-foot units (which is now typical on the West Coast), such volumes would generate hundreds of truck trips per day over nearby highways, since containers must be drayed in both directions. In addition, such a terminal would likely generate multiple doublestack train departures each week, requiring up to 400 additional truck trips for each train. The fact that traffic flows are not always even, and that often most of the volume is concentrated in a three-day period – the day before the ship arrival, the day the ship is in port, and the day after the ship leaves – compounds the problem.

Increased gate activity and movement of vehicles within the marine terminal have forced operators to look closely at land utilization and to develop new terminal design layouts. This, in turn, has given rise to the development of complex inventory control computer systems, some of them incorporating automatic equipment identification (AEI) and position location technology. In some cases design considerations have necessitated a switch from wheeled to stacked operations along with a new system for handling container chassis.

Stacked versus Wheeled Operations

Despite the rapidly increasing cost of waterfront property over the past several years (since international intermodal volumes first began growing significantly), ocean carriers have been demanding larger facilities with space enough to store larger numbers of units and to perform loading and unloading functions faster. Increased volumes have placed a strain on the efficiency of marine terminals, and managers have sought to cope with the problem in essentially two ways.

The first strategy has been to increase stacking heights for containers. Several years ago the conventional wisdom on US West Coast terminal facility design called for four- or five-high stacking of containers in order to achieve maximum density and land utilization. Property costs have remained high, particularly in the high inter-modal throughput ports such as Los Angeles, and this approach has at least enabled terminal operators to help control costs.

But the higher stacking concept has not been without its drawbacks. For example, in five-high blocks, even with overhead lifting capability, more containers have to be moved in order to retrieve "buried" units. Moreover, although higher stacking has allowed storage of more containers, it has also led to a commensurate requirement for space to park or stack the additional carrier-owned chassis to put them on. These factors, when combined with additional handling equipment costs, increased man-hours and the problems associated with keeping client inventories separate, have contributed to the perception that there is a limit to the height containers can be stacked, both safely and economically. As a consequence, a second approach, and one which appears to be gaining in popularity today, has been the shift from a stacked to a wheeled operation.

Studies reportedly used by one major carrier indicate that wheeled operations are significantly less costly than the most common form of stacked operation, even when the capital and operating costs of the larger required chassis fleet are considered. Many carriers have developed a preference for loading containers directly from ship to chassis, if only because it keeps handling down to a minimum.

Yet the handling efficiencies of the wheeled operation (at least in the intermodal context) do not solve the problems caused by separate carrier-owned chassis fleets. If, for example, a Sea-Land container must be married with a Sea-Land chassis, other available empty chassis are not being utilized. This situation has led some observers to estimate that chassis are 50% in oversupply at present, a figure that assumes significantly higher utilization can be achieved based on pooling or similar concepts. Others are more conservative in their estimate of the oversupply. Few dispute, however, that chassis are in abundance in most ports and that equipment routinely stands idle between ship sailings and arrivals, using up valuable acreage which could be used for other terminal functions.

Chassis Pools

Not surprisingly, increasing numbers of rail and marine terminal operators are looking at the chassis pool as a means of increasing productivity, especially by avoiding the problems of having to match containers and chassis according to their respective owners. And this strategy has its supporters among the steamship lines, which, after all, end up paying the big share of chassis acquisition and maintenance costs. In the words of a Sea-Land Service official, "We don't need any more chassis, but we do need to find a way to use that common asset."

Without doubt the use of container chassis has

changed dramatically, reflecting port and railroad determination to keep up with the pace of intermodal movements. Many terminal operators have taken control of chassis operations, leasing hundreds of chassis units to create a "pool" of equipment for exclusive use by their steamship line clients.

The operation of a chassis pool is relatively simple. Equipment is committed to a terminal facility and used by its clients on an as-needed basis. Typically, the lessor will handle all the administrative functions of the pool and arrange for the maintenance and repair of equipment when needed. The rate charged to the customer is an all-in daily rate covering administrative cost, insurance, and, usually, specified types of minor damage or a maximum dollar amount for damages. For example, the lessor might "insure" the first $25. of damages, or simply absorb the cost of repairing lights and flat tires or replacing missing lenses and other particular items.

This is the typical model, although there are some deviations from it. In some cases the chassis are actually leased by the terminal on a long-term basis and then subleased to the terminal users. There are also differences in the way the damage and repair aspects of neutral pools are handled. Some lessors do not absorb any damage expense, however minor. Others might cover all damage but ask the steamship line to subrogate their right to third party claims. In this situation, the lessor reserves the right to bill truckers and other parties responsible for damaging equipment while under their control.

However these arrangements are made, the intermodal customer is assured of chassis equipment whenever needed and it ends up with comparatively few headaches when it comes to maintenance and repair.

The concept of pooling container chassis is not new. In the 1960s the creation of neutral chassis pools to meet shipper and carrier demand enjoyed considerable popularity and played an important role in accelerating the growth of containerization in North America. But after an initial period of development, many major carriers developed strategies based on equipment ownership and began bringing logistics management operations in-house as a means of controlling the (perceived) soaring costs of leasing. As a consequence, interest in chassis pools declined dramatically, particularly in the steamship line sector. Up until a few years ago, only comparatively small inland intermodal pool operations survived, stocked by major chassis lessors such as Flexi-Van, XTRA, Transamerica Container Leasing, and Interpool. The latest resurgence of the neutral pool concept can be directly attributed to increased intermodal activity, particularly the influx of doublestack operations.

But to conclude that a chassis pool run in conjunction with a wheeled operation is the perfect solution to terminal operators' land problems would probably be inaccurate. Chassis pools have substantial advantages for the stacked operation as well. By allowing more efficient movement of container loads in and out of the terminal gate, the incorporation of a neutral pool into the stacked terminal operation can produce land savings in excessof that required to park the chassis fleet. Moreover, strictly speaking, the number of pooled chassis required to meet the peak requirements of all the terminal's customers ought to be significantly lower than when carrier chassis are used.

Although neutral chassis pools at rail terminals do not eliminate drayage, they may substantially reduce its cost by eliminating bare chassis movements. The rail neutral chassis pool was introduced by Burlington Northern to expedite the handling of doublestack trains in Chicago. Ocean carriers with containers on BN trains need not provide chassis for delivery from Chicago: chassis move to and from BN's Cicero yard as needed. Santa Fe has started a neutral chassis pool for its Chicago operation, and now has a neutral pool at its Los Angeles facilities. Chassis for the Los Angeles/Long Beach pool are maintained at a central yard and dispatched as needed to either marine terminals (for imports) or the Santa Fe yard (for exports). If this arrangement succeeds in reducing bare chassis movements, the use of neutral chassis pools can be expected to spread.

In terms of future port markets, the neutral pool concept has most applicability in the multi-user ocean terminal facility, and its growth may be limited to that sector. In carrier operated port terminals, leased pools appear to have less of a role to play, unless the carrier is unable to find appropriate financing for an owned fleet. If railroads choose to become major owners of or lessor/lessees of chassis equipment then leased neutral pools at dedicated intermodal ramps may become obsolete.

Another factor lies in the structure of the chassis leasing industry itself. The concentration of most of North America's chassis in the hands of a decreasing number of companies may have a positive or negative effect on carrier and terminal operator acceptance of the pool concept. At present the major chassis providers are Flexi-Van Leasing, Interpool, Transamerica Container Leasing, Itel, Trac Leasing, Strick Corporation and Trans Ocean Leasing. XTRA, it appears, will also remain in the chassis business through its rail division, which operates a pool for Santa Fe in Chicago.

Overweight Containers

Whether run in conjunction with a wheeled or stacked terminal operation, chassis pools can also limit exposure to liability for chassis-related accidents such as those involving allegedly overweight containers. Overweight containers and chassis maintenance have caused considerable controversy among port managers, highway administrators and even congressional legislators. Both concerns are significant in the debate about how the intermodal revolution has affected the highway infrastructure.

Interest in this area is not surprising when one considers the amount of attention highway safety has received in newspapers and on television. As a result, many aspects of highway transportation in the United States are today being closely examined by legislators. Although much of the attention has been on the long-haul trucking industry, intermodal drayage operators and the steamship lines that employ them have also been affected.

Trade groups representing terminal, ocean and motor carrier interests have become particularly active in this area. For example, the National Association of Stevedores (NAS) and Steamship Operators Intermodal Committee (SOIC), the latter largely through its Atlantic Regional Committee (ARC), have been especially vocal about the relationship between economic deregulation and truck safety. ARC's Newsletter (1988 October issue) contains a lengthy analysis of various views on the subject, but it generally supports the view that market forces provide more than adequate mechanisms to ensure safe truck and chassis operations. And, in cooperation with the Bi-State Harbor Carriers Conference (B-SHCC), an association of truckers serving the area in and around the port areas of New Jersey and New York, SOIC-ARC has organized a series of one-day workshops on issues relating to chassis operations. The first, held in April 1987, discussed tires and tire maintenance. The second, in November 1987, explored the issue of equipment interchange. Both these workshops were intended to educate and generally increase operator awareness of problems arising in the use of intermodal chassis. The significant fact, though, and one which counters the view that drayage and steamship line industries have been inattentive to the problems of chassis operations, is that these workshops have been organized at all. Clearly there is a growing willingness among diverse groups to co-operate in such areas.

Truckers and steamship lines disagree as far as the related problems of overweight containers and chassis maintenance are concerned. Some observers point out the unfairness of situations whereby truck firms are fined for use of poorly maintained equipment or pulling illegal overweight loads, or where they are expected to repair equipment they did not own.

The SOIC has responded to these claims first by questioning the assertion that lines force truckers to accept unsafe equipment. Moreover, SOIC notes that Federal regulations do place the burden of inspection on the trucker and that members of SOIC frequently comment on the cursory and haphazard nature of drivers' inspections at marine terminals. And as far as overweight containers are concerned, while SOIC admits that the "per container" rates used by some shipping conferences may provide an incentive to overload containers, just as significant is the fact that many foreign countries simply have different regulations governing gross vehicle weight limitations and axle loadings.

The guidelines for determining whether a load falls within the legal weight limitations are obscure conditions relating to the minimum distance between the rear tandem of the chassis and the rear tandem of the tractor unit for a given load. The rules are based on standards developed by the American Association of State Highway and Transportation Officials (AASHTO), and, although individual states may have slightly different standards for the construction of state-funded highways, historically the AASHTO rules have been considered a standard for the construction of most of the Interstate highway system.

Given the virtually limitless number of tare weights (both chassis and container), cargo capacities, chassis sizes (length), tractor weights and axle settings, the calculation of whether a load is legal is a difficult one at best. Many overseas shippers are simply unable to fully understand the requirements, particularly since, in many cases, a container may not be, itself, overweight (i.e., over the International Standards Organization 24 ton rating for a 20-foot unit) but the combined weight of the chassis and the container, at least in some axle configurations, renders the load illegal. And compounding the problem, according to the SOIC, are the actions of political jurisdictions who grant excess weight permits in the interests of port competition. This issue has arisen recently in relation to the ports of Oakland and Baltimore, both of which have issued overweight container permits for the carriage of heavy loads over restricted highways in their respective jurisdictions.

Policies of this sort, although they may allow port area motor carriers to avoid highway inspections and fines, present a problem for steamship lines. A port's willingness to accept the movement of heavy units (justified in most cases by research and testing to demonstrate the ability of the roadway in question to bear the additional loads) certainly encourages shippers to overload containers. But since many units are now moving to inland locations, the overweight permits really only pass responsibility along mini- and micro-bridge routes to other jurisdictions where roads may not be constructed to the same tolerances.

Some truckers are concerned about permit systems, however, because if they are issued in a blanket manner, a trucker might unknowingly load a chassis beyond the manufacturer's specification on tires or axles. In the words of one motor carrier executive, "we cannot have states and ports competing for a disaster."

The problems associated with chassis maintenance and the increasing occurrence of overweight container loading is likely to keep motor carriers, ports and steamship lines at odds with each other for a while. Meanwhile, legislators can no longer ignore the issue. Interestingly, one direction federal authorities may want to take is to develop and enforce national standards for the maintenance and repair of chassis equipment.

Railroad Clearances

The major short-term rail infrastructure issue to have emerged as a result of the intermodal revolution is that of railroad line clearances. Doublestack cars require greater overhead clearances than other types of railroad freight cars, and there are many rail routes where tunnels, bridges, overpasses or other structures do not have sufficient clearance. The problem is more common in the eastern states, where the older rail and road infrastructure has for many years limited the use of conventional piggyback cars and tri-level autoracks. Ironically, the well-type Budd Lo-Pac 2000 doublestack car was originally designed as a means of moving piggyback trailers through low eastern clearances. When double-stack cars are loaded with two high-cube, 9-foot, 6-inch high containers, the problem is exacerbated.

The problem reaches its greatest dimensions when 53-foot long, 102-inch-wide domestic containers are placed on top, increasing the lateral clearance requirements at the greatest height. The largest combination requires nearly 10 feet of width at 20 feet above the rail. Few railroad tunnels were built with such clearances, and potential clearance problems with the largest domestic containers are common throughout the rail system.

Ocean carriers, railroads and ports have a common interest in improved clearances and unrestricted double-stack access. The situation, however, is often described as a chicken-and-egg problem: Railroads are generally willing to invest in clearance improvements if traffic to justify that investment is committed, but ocean carriers are unwilling to commit traffic unless clearances are improved. In at least one case, a railroad, an ocean carrier and a port have jointly funded tunnel clearance improvements. Union Pacific, American President and the Port of Oakland have jointly funded tunnel-clearance improvements in the Feather River Canyon. This cooperative action has encouraged other railroads and ports to explore the possibilities of joint endeavors, and at least two similar projects are currently under consideration.

Port Competition

It is doubtful that increased port competition would be judged an unfortunate consequence of intermodal development. Indeed, by some observers, it has been counted as something to be proud of, the healthy sign of an industry emerging from a period of dangerous complacency. And there is no doubt that intermodalism has revitalized certain aspects of the port industry, especially in attracting capital for terminal improvements, creating jobs and furthering regional economic expansion.

Intermodalism and the competition it has produced may have brought out both the best and the worst in port management, however. Certainly the new thinking about terminal design, the use of chassis assets and spectacular changes in crane technology may be counted as important advances for the industry. But at the same time the overweight container controversy and the general "politicization" of the port business may well have public repercussions port administrators did not bargain for.

Generally speaking, in the rush to position themselves competitively, and with the carrier community increasingly calling the shots, many port managers have developed a very different view of their role in an organization vested with the authority and responsibility for developing what is, essentially, a public resource. The picture is more one of a "them or us" race in which capturing a key steamship line account might mean the difference between success or failure for an executive. And with overriding personal interests of this sort in operation, legislators will need to pay close attention to port development as it relates to intermodalism.

Rail Intermodal Hubs

The "pig ramp" has fallen victim to the intermodal revolution. As piggyback service expanded in the 1950s and 1960s, railroads established hundreds of piggyback terminals, most of them nothing more than concrete or gravel ramps where TOFC cars could be circus-loaded using truck tractors. In many cases, these "pig ramps" were simply added to existing team tracks or quickly built in a corner of a freight yard. Investment was minimal, but the traffic was minimal too.

Yet as late as 1974, U.S. railroads still had some 1,500 pig ramps (Figure 5-3), of which only 105 had acquired mechanical lift capability. The other 1,400-odd "terminals" were low volume pig ramps that still circus-loaded traffic, if they had any traffic at all. By 1984, the situation had changed drastically. Over a thousand pig ramps were closed, and those judged to be worth keeping were being given mechanical lift equipment. By 1989, the network was being condensed to 200-300 terminals. Most of the remaining terminals had mechanical lift equipment, and it is clear that in just a few more years all the terminals still operating will be mechanized.

The pig ramp is gone, and has been replaced by the intermodal hub. The old piggyback hands that used to "chain 'em down" would scarcely recognize the new facilities. Spacious, paved, lighted and dominated by massive machinery, today's intermodal hubs have nearly become machines themselves, dedicated to achieving levels of efficient throughput unimagined by the most optimistic planners of the 1960s.

The replacement of primitive ramps with mechanized hubs and the growth of inland container

US Rail Intermodal Terminals

	Total Terminals	Mechanized Terminals
1974	1,500	105
1984	430	150
1989 est.	300	215

Source: Greenbrier Intermodal

Figure 5-3

movements by rail have been simultaneous. Major railroad terminals have long had gantry cranes to transfer heavy freight to and from flatcars and gondolas. Some early attempts at LCL containerization used overhead gantries to transfer the containers to trucks. It was a short step to adapt those gantries to handle piggyback trailers. Santa Fe's Corwith Yard, for many years the busiest piggyback terminal in the country, received its first specially built gantry crane in 1964. Later, some enterprising soul modified a log-handling loader to lift trailers, and the sideloader or "Piggypacker" began to roam the intermodal terminals.

Besides the efficiency that gantries and sideloaders brought to piggyback operations, they made it possible to move containers on flatcars without chassis (COFC). Formerly, the few containers that moved by rail were carried with chassis as TOFC traffic, surrendering some of the potential efficiency of containerization. Mechanical lift capability made possible the growth of mini-landbridge movements, starting in 1972. Thereafter, any railroad that wanted to participate in the growth of inland container traffic had to mechanize its critical intermodal facilities, even if its piggyback business could get along with circus loading.

Mechanized lift also allowed the design of third-generation intermodal equipment, with the linehaul capacity and efficiency that equipment provides. Articulated equipment such as the Impack car does not have a continuous platform for circus loading, and the single-unit Front Runner and its kin lack bridgeplates or any other means to unload at a ramp. Articulated doublestack cars would be doubly impossible without mechanical lift equipment.

Even the Trailer train flatcar fleet has been largely stripped of bridgeplates, making service at the few remaining pig ramps harder and harder.

Lift equipment is expensive, with sideloaders and gantries going for $500,000 to $1,200,000 each. Railroads prudently concentrated their investment in lift equipment at the busiest intermodal terminals, the future hubs. At the same time, mergers and system rationalization were concentrating intermodal traffic on fewer routes and at fewer terminals. The dedicated trains and fast schedules required to compete for intermodal traffic would not tolerate stops for set-outs at a myriad of intermediate points. The railroads, like other transportation modes, were moving toward a hub and spoke system.

The hub and spoke system that has emerged depends critically on the efficiency of draymen and regional trucking firms. While the linehauls and hubs are operated by the railroads, the spokes are highways reaching out for traffic 250 miles or more away. A major rail hub can serve a substantial territory with this kind of trucking extension. Figure 5-4 shows the location of hubs with stack-train service in 1988. It is clear from the map that there are few major US population centers outside the reach of those hub and spoke operations.

Looking at the map of intermodal hubs, or the maps of intermodal routes in Chapter 4, it is easy to forget that intermodal carriers are competing in a door-to-door market. Both doors are likely to be some distance from rail intermodal terminals, so it is not enough to provide fast and efficient linehaul rail service. Rail equipment must be loaded and unloaded quickly and efficiently in the

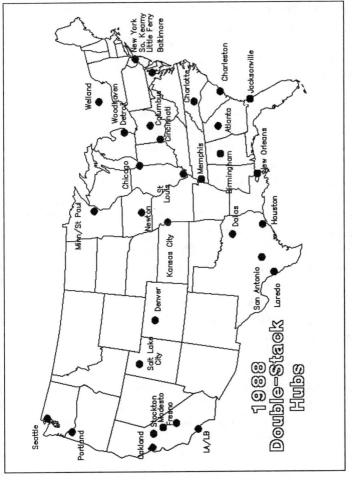

1988
Double-Stack Hubs

Seattle
Portland
Oakland
Stockton
Modesto
Fresno
LA/LB
Salt Lake City
Denver
San Antonio
Laredo
Kansas City
Minn/St Paul
Newton
Dallas
Houston
Chicago
St Louis
Memphis
Birmingham
New Orleans
Welland
Woodhaven
Detroit
Columbus
Cincinnati
Charlotte
Atlanta
Charleston
Jacksonville
New York
So. Kearny
Little Ferry
Baltimore

Figure 5-4

terminals, and the trailer or container taken from and handed to local truckers with a minimum of delay and paperwork.

More and more often, the work of an intermodal terminal begins well before the shipment arrives. The first and last contacts for an intermodal movement are likely to be electronic. Besides saving on the cost of paperwork, electronic data interchange (EDI) in any of its many forms serves as an outreach for the intermodal terminal.

Anyone who spends time at an intermodal terminal – rail or marine – will be struck by the time and effort consumed in gate operations, and the precious space consumed by parking trailers and containers on chassis. If a trailer or container arrives off the street with no advance notice, it must be inspected, a bill of lading must be issued, a waybill must be created, and the unit must be parked until assigned to a railcar and loaded. At the other end of the movement, the unit must be parked while the consignee is notified and makes arrangements to pick it up. This is a recipe for congestion and inefficiency. Moreover, the busiest hubs could never handle their current and future throughput under a manual system.

With EDI, information on the shipment precedes the shipment itself, allowing the terminal and the railroad to plan. Indeed, once the information is available electronically, most of the routine planning can be done automatically, by computer. When an EDI shipment arrives at the gate, its paperwork is already done and the truck driver can be directed to a waiting railcar and lift machine. The goal at new facilities is to get the truck driver in and out in 15 minutes, and the EDI outreach makes it possible.

The newest facilities, like BN's Seattle International Gateway or SP's ICTF in Los Angeles, have been designed for EDI from the start. These new hubs can minimize the space devoted to parking, and the space and labor devoted to long gate routines.

EDI and the railroad's own information systems are as large a part of terminal operations as gantries, gates and parking. The terminal staff must blend and balance the elements, and deal with the inevitable unexpected complications.

Much of the success or failure of rail intermodal operations depends on hub terminal management. Fast, competitive schedules and high equipment utilization both depend on the terminal to turn the train quickly. Terminal costs are a large part of the total rail expense, and terminal managers are called on to squeeze every dime. Door-to-door service quality depends on the ability of terminal managers to dispatch and receive shipments promptly. Finally, the terminal is a critical focus for control of shipment loss and damage.

Increasingly, railroads have organized intermodal terminals differently from freight yards and other facilities. Sometimes separate business units are set up to operate intermodal yards, such as the former Western Pacific's "Feather River Intermodal Services Company" ("FRISCO") Others have assigned the task to trucking subsidiaries, such as SP's Pacific Motor Transport.

One recent trend is the operation of rail hubs by independent contractors. Besides bringing experience and expertise, independent contractors sometimes also bring the ability to negotiate new, more efficient work rules designed for intermodal operations. Some rail facilities are now operated by Teamsters, rather than by rail union labor, under arrangements with independent contractors.

Even with the number of rail intermodal terminals cut from 1,500 to less than 300, there is still a wide range of sizes and configurations. Moreover, the largest and busiest hubs are concentrated in a few major metropolitan areas.

Chicago has always figured prominently in the railroad industry, and it retains that prominence for intermodal traffic. As an origin and destination, Chicago not only serves as the hub for the upper Midwest and much of the Great Lakes industrial region, but is also home to many major third party intermodal customers – freight forwarders, shipper's associations, consolidators, and shipper's agents – who together account for a large part of all intermodal traffic. Most major steamship lines maintain container yards or other facilities in the Chicago area (although the increased use of chassis pools has reduced their importance). As a gateway and interchange point, Chicago is served directly by six of the seven largest railroads (SP serves Chicago indirectly via connections with Soo Line and BN; UP has direct access but moves most intermodal traffic over its CNW connection), and several large regionals. The two largest rail intermodal traffic flows are between Chicago and Los Angeles, and Chicago and New York. Of the 20 busiest intermodal routes in 1987, Chicago figured in all but three.

Santa Fe's Corwith yard in Chicago was for many years the nation's busiest, with 128 acres of land and eight gantry cranes. But Corwith is only one of a ring of intermodal yards serving Chicago, which include the facilities of BN (93 acres and five lifts at Cicero), Conrail (three yards with 10 lifts among them), CSX (two yards totaling over 70 acres and at least five lifts), GTW (33 acres and six lifts), IC (46 acres, three lifts), NS (former NW facilities with three lifts), and Soo (the former MILW yard with 47 acres and at least four lifts).

Chicago and North Western is a special case, because besides a major Chicago-area facility at Proviso (20 acres, two lifts), CNW operates Global 1, the first inland intermodal facility designed and built especially to handle doublestack trains. In mid-1985, soon after APL had established stack trains converging on CNW from Los Angeles, Seattle and New York, CNW decided to convert its Wood St. yard and nearby property for the exclusive purpose of originating, terminating, transferring and interchanging stack trains. To that end CNW spent $28 million on Global 1 itself and another $8 million on approaches and related work. A large part of that total was invested in four Mi-Jack gantry cranes with a 71-foot span and the unique ability to turn containers 180 degrees and lift them over a loaded doublestack car. Tracks were spaced to allow loading and unloading stack cars to and from chassis, flatcars or other stack cars. CNW officials referred to the new facility as "a turning basin for doublestack trains," accurately describing the task Global 1 was designed to accomplish.

Early in 1989, the stage was set for the next development in Chicago. United Parcel Service, the nation's largest TOFC shipper, announced plans to build a massive distribution hub near Chicago where a General Motors Fisher Body plant now stands. As part of this project, Santa Fe plans to convert an adjacent rail facility to a dedicated UPS intermodal yard at a cost of $40 million. Although not large as intermodal hubs go, this facility will be the first built for an individual shipper. In a sense, this inland development parallels the trend toward on-dock port facilities.

In Los Angeles, at the other end of the heaviest intermodal traffic flow, is Southern Pacific's Intermodal Container Transfer Facility (ICTF), now the largest intermodal facility in the world and with further expansion under way. The 150-acre ICTF was dedicated in January 1987 after an eight-year planning and construction effort and an expenditure of $80 million. At 1.3 miles long, the ICTF can hold 250 conventional flatcars or 80 doublestack cars and has 1,600 parking slots. The 16-lane computerized entry gate can process 230 containers per hour. The yard itself has five loading/unloading tracks, each with its own gantry crane. Despite this massive capacity, traffic through the ICTF has grown so rapidly that the second-year volume exceeded the fifth-year projections. The ICTF is filling up fast. SP added 87 acres to the facility far sooner than anyone had imagined, and has designated 55 more acres for future expansion.

The greatest success of the ICTF, however, is its EDI outreach and its computerized operating system. SP has been a pioneer in EDI, with over 50% of its business handled electronically by early 1989. Implementation of EDI and computerized gates allow the ICTF to accept most inbound traffic with a simple verification of container initials and number. Draymen can be directed to a railcar ready for the box, rather than parking or waiting. Although not every shipment is handled that fast, the ICTF works to a 15-minute standard.

The rapid growth of intermodal traffic and the high standards being set for service and efficiency require the railroads to continually upgrade their facilities, and intermodal facility improvements are prominent in capital investment plans. Every major railroad is adding acreage, lift machines, tracks or whole new facilities. Even the regional railroads are investing in intermodal, from new yards on the Wisconsin Central to a sideloader on tiny Stockton Terminal & Eastern.

With the rising complexity of intermodal transportation and the blurring of traditional roles, it should not be surprising that ocean carriers, their subsidiaries, and even a port have opened inland rail facilities.

Both APL and Sea-Land operate their own land-side rail terminals in New Jersey, APL's at South Kearny and Sea-Land's at North Bergen. APL's sister organization, American President Intermodal, now operates a rail terminal at Woodhaven, Mich., to support its new Detroit-Chicago-Dallas doublestack service. Rail-Bridge Corp., a subsidiary of K-Line, operates two inland rail hubs, one in Elizabeth, N.J., and a second in Welland, Ont.

Perhaps the boldest inland marine development is the Virginia Inland Port (VIP), in Front Royal, VA. VIP will be a rail intermodal terminal surrounded by distribution centers, offices and related facilities over a hundred miles inland from the Hampton Roads ports. The initial terminal occupies 45 acres of the 162 acre site. VIP will be connected to the ports by dedicated Norfolk Southern intermodal trains.

Future Infrastructure Development

The complexity of intermodal operations calls for one kind of flexibility – the ability of a facility or system

201

of facilities to handle the full range of intermodal operations efficiently. The commitments and risks involved in intermodal planning call for another kind of flexibility – the ability to progress, and to remain competitive in a highly competitive industry, and still accommodate a dimly seen future.

Intermodal growth, by virtue of its complexity and dynamism, demands both kinds of flexibility. In those circumstances, port planning gains both a spatial and a time dimension. Port planning must extend beyond the terminal gates, and it must accommodate and shape the future. Meanwhile railroads will need to be responsive to the needs of both domestic and international shippers, upgrading facilities, track and tunnels to accommodate the demands of increasing intermodal volumes. Last but not least, state and federal administrators will have to come to terms wtih highway weight limits and provide a way out of the overweight crisis.

Transportation executives and their regulatory counterparts need to take a long, hard look at just how port, rail, and highway resources are going to be most efficiently exploited as the intermodal revolution continues.

Chapter 6

INTERMODAL MARKETING AND MANAGEMENT

Intermodal Cooperation

Before the intermodal revolution, there was rarely a need for cooperation among ports, ocean carriers and railroads. Before ocean carrier services were extended inland over the rails, direct contact between ocean carriers and railroads was uncommon. But growth in inland intermodal traffic has made port choice discretionary for large volumes of containerized cargo, giving the ports an incentive to involve themselves in transportation matters beyond their terminal boundaries.

It was years before the introduction of doublestack trains that ports, ocean carriers and railroads began to carry large volumes of high-priority container traffic that required careful cooperation. The advent of those large-scale intermodal services has altered traditional relationships. Railroads scrambled to accommodate container traffic, paying attention first to basic problems such as car supply, mechanical lift equipment and chassis parking at terminals.

A Growing Need

The expansion of doublestack service has multiplied the traffic affected by port, ocean carrier and railroad cooperation. That cooperation resulted in a higher standard of service and an opportunity for cost savings. In particular, three major factors create a growing need for cooperation between ports, ocean carriers and railroads.

First is the discretionary nature of inland container flows. Routing of containers bound to or from inland rail hubs has become discretionary because intermodal cargo can move efficiently to major inland points from more than one competing port, and because extension of ocean carrier services inland has shifted routing decisions from ocean shipper to ocean carrier. Ocean carriers in the Transpacific trade can reach Chicago, Kansas City or St. Louis with comparable costs and service from any major West Coast port. Ocean carriers in the Atlantic trades can do the same from several East Coast ports. This flexibility allows ocean carriers to shift between competing ports for better intermodal facilities, lower transfer costs or a better contract offer from a different railroad. The ocean carriers' flexibility leads the ports, and the railroads that serve them, to compete more intensely. Load centering, the practice of funneling both local and inland traffic through a small number of container ports, has raised the stakes even further, so ports are increasingly competing for large inland flows on an "all or nothing" basis.

A second factor in the need for increased cooperation between ports, ocean carriers and railroads is the increased use of multi-year contracts. Deregulation and regulatory exemption of intermodal traffic have had numerous effects, including the shift from published tariffs to negotiated contracts. The use of contracts rather than tariffs allows ocean carriers and railroads to enter into multi-year commitments regarding volume, rates and service, and to either benefit from cooperation or suffer from its lack. Once such a commitment is made, carriers can plan and invest to handle a specific minimum volume of traffic. The contract commitment directs traffic through a specific port for a period of up to five years, and requires the cooperation of that port for success in the intermodal market.

Intensified competition on land, at sea and between ports is the third factor that necessitates cooperation among all three parties. Market pressure from deregulated trucks has added to the railroad competition encouraged by the Staggers Act and the exemption from regulation granted by the ICC to intermodal traffic. Intermodal shippers can often dray their freight to competing intermodal yards. Rail mergers have created large intermodal systems, offering multiple competing routes between major origins and destinations. Third parties have also encouraged competition, because third parties themselves are highly competitive and often have enough traffic to negotiate favorable contracts. Recent large increases in ocean carrier container capacity have also given ocean carriers incentives for aggressive pricing. Changes in the conference system, notably the increased latitude for "independent action," have brought much the same competitive pressure on the sea as deregulation has on land.

Effects Of The Revolution

Some aspects of the ocean carrier/port relationship have been significantly altered by the intermodal revolution. Unlike the traditional imports and exports of the port hinterland, inland intermodal cargo is fundamentally discretionary, giving ocean carriers substantial freedom in the choice of a load center port. This freedom has fueled greater competition between ports in different regions, as well as between ports in the same region.

The number of large ocean carriers has been

reduced by merger, service rationalizations and joint ventures, and each remaining carrier acquires greater importance. These large remaining carriers have substantial bargaining leverage in negotiations with ports over terminal size, handling equipment, port charges, intermodal transfer facilities and ancillary port services. To compete, ports continually invest in container cranes, terminal improvements, electronic information systems, and on-dock or near-dock rail transfer facilities, and they seek multi-year ocean carrier commitments to secure these investments.

The ocean carrier/port relationship expands to include the railroads when the ocean carriers or ports take an active part in reducing rail transfer costs or arranging inland transportation. Until ocean carriers began offering inland service on through bills of lading, shippers, receivers or their agents typically chose both port choice and inland routing. Both ports and ocean carriers advertised to inland customers, but ocean carrier and port services ended at the marine terminal gate. The railroads were not involved. Under mini-landbridge tariffs, however, the ocean carrier selects both the port and the inland carrier.

Relations between railroads and ports have long focused on facilities and access issues. These issues have become critical to the future cooperation between railroads and ports, and to the future of intermodalism itself. The issue of rail transfer facilities became relevant when competition led ocean carriers and railroads to seek transfer cost savings. The primary link between ship and rail has been, and continues to be, over-the-road drayage. Elimination of over-the-road drayage through the provision of "on-dock" transfer facilities can confer an advantage to one port and railroad combination in the competiion for ocean carrier business, and force competing carrier and port combinations to seek comparable improvements.

Each major container port has a unique configuration of marine terminals and rail facilities, so the question is not as simple as on-dock versus off-dock. Several ports have examined alternatives designed to reduce transfer costs between existing facilities.

Ports consider the presence of two or more competing railroads an advantage in attracting discretionary cargo. Each port, however, would prefer that those railroads would serve it to the exclusion of all other ports. The railroads prefer to serve as many ports as possible, and to be the only railroad at each. It comes as no surprise, then, that the idea of access for more railroads is applauded by the port and the other railroads, and opposed by other ports and the existing railroad. This dilemma has occurred at one major port, and is likely to occur elsewhere as ports seek to improve rail access and encourage rail competition.

Contractual Relationships

Most of the container traffic between ocean carriers and railroads moves under contract. Some inland traffic is still handled under tariffs, tendered either by ocean carriers or third parties, but the traffic flows on current and potential doublestack operations require contractual relationships. There are three principal types of contracts between ocean carriers and railroads.

Dedicated Train Contracts. The first type is a dedicated stack train operation, the form in which doublestack operations began. In such a contract, the railroad operates a stack train on a fixed route for the exclusive use of the ocean carrier. This may be a "take or pay" contract in which the ocean carrier pays for the round-trip stack train movement, whether or not there are any containers aboard.

Dedicated Car Contracts. A second contract type dedicates a number of stack cars for the use of the ocean carrier, but they operate in regularly scheduled inter-modal or common-user trains rather than by themselves. This type of contract is relatively uncommon, as it has been largely superceded by "common-user" volume contracts.

Common-User Contracts. The third and perhaps most common contract type is the "common-user" volume agreement. In such an agreement, the ocean carrier commits to ship a minimum annual volume of containers over the railroad in exchange for favorable rates. The low rates are typically offered in corridors where regular common-user doublestack trains are operated, although in some cases the commitment is system-wide. The low rates are based on the expected use of stack cars, but in low-volume corridors or where stack cars are in short supply, the containers may actually move on conventional equipment. The rates for common-user volume contracts depend on the traffic volume in question. Some railroads negotiate each volume discount separately, while others have put a "tier" system in place, tying rates to volume thresholds. Such contracts are usually open to large third parties, or to ports acting as shipper's agents.

Since large ocean carriers have container flows in several corridors, such carriers often have several rail

208

contracts. Such a combination may include dedicated train contracts for the largest corridors (such as Los Angeles-Chicago), and one or more common-user contracts for smaller flows.

The Role of Third Parties

Few sectors of the freight transportation industry, either domestic or international, have been affected more by the intermodal revolution than the freight forwarding and brokering business. The growth of so-called "third parties" during the last half of the 1980s was truly remarkable, both in terms of the sheer number of companies that now populate this area of the industry, and in terms of the range of services they provide. According to *The Private Carrier*, between 1980 and 1986, brokers represented the fastest growing segment of transportation, going from just a handful to 6,000 licensed brokers in only six years.

As far as services are concerned, third parties have added every conceivable type of transportation and distribution service to the truck brokering, consolidating, freight bill auditing, and payment services that have traditionally characterized the brokering and forwarding business.

The rapid emergence of a strong third party sector is not surprising given that brokers and forwarders essentially serve both shipper and carrier. The services provided by third parties allow shippers to enjoy lower intermodal rates, while at the same time relieving carriers of the burden of freight consolidation and providing sufficient volumes to make intermodal shipments worthwhile. Without third parties it is arguable that intermodal growth would have been significantly slower than it has been during the 1980s, and that no "revolution" would have occurred.

Nevertheless, the third party industry faces a classic dilemma. Third parties have contributed greatly to the growth of intermodalism, but this very growth has encouraged some carriers to establish a direct relationship with shippers, developing significant marketing operations of their own and becoming in some cases quasi-third parties.

On the ocean carrier side the most widely noted example of this has been the entry of American President Companies into intermodal marketing via its American President Distribution Services subsidiary. An example from the railroad side is Burlington Northern's wholly-owned BN Worldwide service which aims to be a non-asset owning NVOCC-type operation serving a global marketplace. The development of retail strategies such as those by rail and steamship carriers has resulted in a blurring of traditional transportation roles and a tremendous diversity in relationships between railroads and third parties.

Diverse Railroad Strategies

Southern Pacific, Burlington Northern, Santa Fe, Conrail and CSX are among those railroads which have supported third party companies. SP, for example, relies heavily on third parties. Southern Pacific does business with American President and other major transportation companies such as the Hub Group.

The Burlington Northern Railroad regards third

parties as partners in providing its intermodal services and has a stated policy position on its marketing strategy. As a BN executive said, "BN has elected to sell its intermodal transportation services primarily through transportation companies because we recognize wholesalers can provide quality geographic market coverage and customer service." The bulk of BN's intermodal business is wholesale, although it does enjoy a few retail relationships, most notably with the US Postal Service and with United Parcel Service.

On the other hand, railroads such as the Grand Trunk Western, Canadian Pacific, Canadian National and Norfolk Southern seem just as committed to maintaining a direct hold over marketing operations. A relationship GTW developed with Mazda, for example, depended heavily on direct involvement with the customer, prompting a GTW intermodal marketing manager to comment to the *Journal of Commerce* that "a third party can't have the same insight into how we can meet customers' needs."

In Canada the preferred relationship with shippers appears to be a direct one. Both the Canadian National and Canadian Pacific railways have substantial retailing operations and handle all their domestic business without third parties. Brokers are used for transborder business with the United States.

Between Grand Trunk and the Canadian railroads on the one hand, and Southern Pacific and the Burlington Northern on the other, railroads such as the Union Pacific have developed a joint wholesale and retail marketing strategy. Although UP has a reputation as being a retail railroad, in fact 90% of its business is handled by third parties. UP has a substantial relationship with American President Intermodal in the Midwest-Texas corridor, for example, the latter wholesaling its stack train services (which use UP track and terminals) through a wide network of third parties. UP has a retail division, UP Freight Services, which offers door-to-door intermodal service.

Backhauls

Third parties have played a significant role in the solicitation of so-called "backhaul" freight. Since the success of any intermodal transportation system depends heavily on equipment utilization and the ability to reposition containers and trailers, backhaul marketing has come to play an important role in determining the overall economics of intermodalism, especially doublestack service.

The introduction and growth of stack train operations was based initially on international volumes entering the United States through the major California and Washington ocean ports. However, the imbalance between eastbound import cargoes and westbound export cargoes meant that carriers were forced to develop methods for attracting freight moving in the opposite direction. From the beginning, American President Lines took an aggressive approach to the backhaul question, soliciting freight to balance its stack train operation via two subsidiaries of Transway International: Eastern Carloading and Merchant Stor-Dor.

These two companies provided the westbound loads for APL's initial doublestack Liner Train until 1985, when the carrier purchased National Piggyback, the nation's largest intermodal shippers agent. Since that date, further re-organization of American President Companies into distinct units, each handling different aspects of transportation, has placed the National Piggyback operation under the control of American President Domestic, along with American President Intermodal, which is responsible for the trains.

The railroads not only recognize the backhaul problem but also appear prepared to structure their rates to help carriers such as API. Thus while Union Pacific's arrangements with API provide for a round-trip rate (which obligates API to pay for the movement of containers in both directions), they also contain a relatively low "additive" rate for loads (as opposed to empties) in the backhaul direction. API has, therefore, a major incentive to maximize westbound loadings, since any revenues over and above the "additive" rate represents a profit. UP has offered similar contracts to other customers.

Another approach, taken by railroads such as the Burlington Northern, Santa Fe and Southern Pacific, has been to make arrangements with ocean carriers whereby the railroad essentially "buys" the excess westbound capacity back from the ocean carrier in order to market it themselves, usually through third parties.

This represents an attractive compromise for ocean carriers unwilling to purchase domestic shipper's agents or invest in establishing an operation to solicit backhaul loads, especially since it also allows railroads to preserve control over intermodal marketing.

This type of arrangement often consists of a multi-tiered rate structure: one rate for returning empties, one for moving containers with ocean carrier loads and a "management fee" for returning a container with a railroad solicited load. This latter management fee is usually less than the charge for moving an empty container, and the railroads typically agree to return the container to the West Coast within 30 days (often considerably faster than the ocean carriers can get it back themselves).

These "buy back" provisions therefore provide an incentive for the ocean carrier either to solicit exports through their own marketing organizations and to turn over whatever capacity they cannot fill to the railroad, or to simply turn all westbound containers over to the railroad and not bother with inland marketing. Either way, third parties have and will continue to provide a valuable service to rail and ocean carriers.

The Third Party Wedge: The Shipper's Dilemma

Despite the adventures into retailing by some carriers, the third party function has clear legitimacy in the intermodal business. The fact is that not all rail or marine carriers can support a retail operation, and those that can, cannot do so everywhere. Several railroads have stated their preference for a "wholesale" approach and the market has certainly proved open enough for the freight forwarders, NVOCCs, and shipper's agents that now populate the intermodal industry.

However, some observers feel the growth of the third party sector threatens to destabilize the transportation and logistics business, at least from the shipper's perspective. A January 1988 editorial in *Distribution* magazine began by stating "third party logistics services are driving a wedge through the field of transportation and distribution management. Just when it seemed there was a brighter future, and higher status, for traffic

214

professionals within American companies, independent suppliers of logistics services have launched a marketing onslaught which could permanently alter the way many businesses handle their logistics requirements."

The fact is that deregulation and technological advances, especially in the field of computerized information processing, have made logistics and pricing management increasingly complex. And in this environment, the professional distribution broker can often perform services more effectively and less expensively than the shipper's own transportation department. Add to this the *Distribution* editorial comment, "the mesmerizing 'lean and mean' doctrines of today's most fashionable management gurus," and the result is a perception that transportation and distribution departments are a luxury many companies simply cannot afford.

From this standpoint, "third party" may be almost a misnomer, because in many cases they are able to give a customer more 'first person' involvement than ever before. In the burgeoning just-in-time market, third parties are beginning to take on more responsibility for their shipper client's transportation operations, even to the extent of determining the mode to be used, the routing and even the amount of merchandise that is to be shipped.

Without doubt, the intermodal revolution has promoted a huge expansion in the third party sector. This growth is altering the way carriers and shippers see the transportation function. For the carrier, third parties provide a useful (if not indispensable) marketing service, at least for small and medium size shippers. From another viewpoint, however, the extent to which brokers and forwarders are now handling traditional logistics functions is beginning to threaten transportation managers in the shipper community. At stake for both carrier and shipper is control – on the one hand, control over enough freight that carriers may be condemned to operate in a perpetual "buyers market," and on the other, control over so many facets of transportation that shippers will lose their access to modal and pricing alternatives.

Domestic Containerization

Until recently, domestic containerization has had a history of false starts. Periodic attempts to create a domestic rail container system always failed, at least in part because each of them started from scratch with new types of containers, cars and facilities.

It appears that domestic containerization is finally here to stay. Whether it becomes the dominant intermodal system is another matter, but by using existing ISO boxes, doublestack cars and intermodal hubs, and using a sales force of third parties, the current wave of domestic containerization has at last reached the shore. In late 1988, American President Intermodal saw domestic traffic pass its record-breaking international traffic for the first time. The CSX/Sea-Land merger has spawned CSLI, offering nationwide domestic container service. BN has formed its own subsidiary, BN America, without ocean carrier involvement, to pursue domestic container traffic on the BN system and beyond.

The Canadian experience has been different. In 1979, Canadian Pacific began converting its intermodal business to 44-foot, 3-inch containers designed especially for domestic traffic. Subsequently, CP also began loading empty import ISO containers with backhaul domestic freight. As a result, containers dominate domestic intermodal traffic on one of Canada's two nationwide systems. Canadian National has continued to promote its trailer system.

Successful US domestic containerization began with APL's efforts to fill import containers that would otherwise return to the West Coast empty. Even before APL began using doublestacks, the best export solicitation efforts could not balance the imports.

The use of doublestack trains brought the matter to a head in two ways. First, the greater capacity of stack trains increased the need for backhaul loads. Second, APL contracted to buy round-trip rail transportation from UP, and supplied its own cars. The contract charged a higher rate for loaded versus empty backhauls, but the incremental cost was less than APL's potential backhaul revenue. This created an opportunity to earn profits and a powerful incentive for APL, and later API, to fill the backhauls. Indeed, APL's developing doublestack inland services could offer highly competitive eastbound rates because APL counted on the backhaul traffic to pull its own weight and contribute to overall profitability. From the first experimental stack train movement in 1983, APL had already arranged backhaul loads with Chicago-area shipper's agents.

APL made its backhaul arrangements permanent in 1985, when it bought National Piggyback, the country's largest shipper's agent. National Piggyback has been integrated into American President Companies, and although it still continues a substantial trailer business, one of its primary functions is soliciting domestic traffic for API's doublestack trains.

Domestic containerization took another leap forward when API and its subsidiaries began soliciting domestic traffic in both directions, not merely as backhaul traffic, and introduced containers designed for domestic loading only. APL had already introduced 45-foot containers to international service. The domestic containers API bought were 48 feet long, 9-feet 6-inches high, and 102 inches wide, breaking with ISO standards for container dimensions. The 48-footers were designed with multiple corner castings to stack with 40-foot and 45-foot containers on trains. The new domestic boxes gave API a cubic capacity competitive with long-haul trucks, and more than competitive with the general run of piggyback trailers.

The 48 x 102 container has become a *de facto* standard for domestic use, with other ocean carriers, leasing companies and even railroads acquiring similar units. APL, now APC, has also purchased a number of 53-foot containers for low-density freight, but those containers are not yet highway-legal in all states.

Although other major steamship lines have established North American subsidiaries to handle their inland intermodal traffic, for the most part they have not directly participated in the domestic market. They are, however, participating by using railroad buyback programs. When the railroads assume the burden of filling backhaul capacity, they typically resell the capacity wholesale to third parties who fill the boxes with domestic loads.

Following the CSX/Sea-Land merger, CSX/Sea-Land Intermodal (CSLI) was created to integrate the inland

Figure 6-1 American President Companies' 48-foot x 102-inch-wide domestic containers. Courtesy American President Companies.

intermodal activities of Sea-Land with CSX's own inter-modal services and marketing. Surprisingly enough, but in fitting with CSLI's nationwide charter, the initial service and marketing targets were well beyond the CSX system, using western railroad connections to offer service between Los Angeles and Atlanta, and Los Angeles and Chicago. CSLI added several hundred domestic containers to Sea-Land's fleet to support domestic service. CSX Container Services operates container depots and repair facilities at key points in the CSX service territory, and is expanding to keep pace with CSLI. CMX, CSX's nationwide drayage operator (mostly through contracts), is likewise expanding to support CSLI services.

The newest player in domestic containerization is BN America, a separate business unit of BN charged with developing domestic container traffic – first on the BN system, and eventually beyond. BN's domestic containers were initially put into service between Denver and Dallas, a shorter haul than typical transcontinental backhauls in marine containers. BNA has also added its containers to BN's Expediter trains. During 1989 BNA launched an aggressive expansion of its network with plans to have broad coverage across the BN system by the end of the year.

The Chassis Puzzle

Early discussions of domestic containerization ap-plauded the potential for linehaul savings, but lamented the seemingly unsolvable problem of chassis logistics.

From the perspective of 1970, chassis logistics would indeed seem an insuperable problem. Intermodal operations were conducted from over a thousand ramps, some of them literally no more than gravel ramps at weed-grown team tracks. The notion of supplying and maintaining railroad-owned chassis at all or even most such locations would be daunting to the most ardent intermodal advocate. Capital, storage and maintenance costs would have been high, utilization nil.

By the late 1980s, several developments had improved the outlook. Hundreds of small ramps were closed, and operations were concentrated at major hubs with mechanical lift capability. The enormous increases in inland rail movements of marine containers without chassis led most major steamship companies to establish their own chassis fleets at major hubs. Although chassis maintenance remains a high-cost item for all intermodal carriers, the expansion of contract maintenance facilities has made costs more predictable and logistics less of a headache. Chassis-handling machines (chassis flippers) and vertical storage racks have reduced the tendency of chassis fleets to consume valuable terminal space.

The neutral chassis pool has been an important part of the solution to this puzzle. By establishing one fleet to serve multiple international clients, the neutral chassis pool boosts utilization and brings unit maintenance and storage costs into line. Moreover, it relieves individual intermodal operators of fleet management and logistics chores. The first neutral chassis pools were established for international traffic, but were soon employed in domestic service as well.

Looking into the 1990s, chassis logistics are still a problem for domestic container services, as they are for inland international services, but the problem no longer appears so great. The industry needs better chassis information and tracking systems, for control of chassis utilization has emerged as a major issue. Automatic Equipment Identification is a long-awaited development, and may provide one of the few remaining pieces to the chassis puzzle.

Boxcars To Boxes?

For decades, the 40-foot boxcar was the standard rail vehicle. There are strong indications that a domestic container may emerge as the standard rail vehicle for future non-bulk movements, leading some observers to proclaim the obsolescence of boxcars. Under the generally valid assumption that what moves in a boxcar can move in a box, will the remaining boxcar traffic be converted to boxes?

Both the boxcar fleet and the traffic it carries took a nosedive in the 1970s. The traffic went to trucks and to piggyback, but most of all it went to jumbo covered hoppers, because in the early 1970s much of the fleet consisted of older 40-foot boxcars held in reserve for the peak grain harvest. Wholesale scrapping of these cars led to the "boxcar shortage," the creation of incentive per diem, and the flood of investor-owned plain boxcars. The entry of Railbox and the recession of 1982-83 turned the shortage to a glut, and boxcars were stored by the thousands.

Then, as the economy recovered, boxcar traffic recovered as well, and by the end of the 1980s boxcar utilization rates had stabilized at acceptable levels. The small declines between 1985 and 1988 likely have as much to do with plant closings and branchline abandonments as with the boxcar's ability to compete in the present market. That market is concentrated in heavy industrial goods, especially intermediate products such as lumber, paper and auto parts, and in factory-to-warehouse movements of appliances and canned foods. In those markets, the boxcar has become integrated into the production and distribution chain. Some paper plants actually extend the production line conveyors through the car doors.

The boxcar survives because it is plentiful and cheap. Also, many of the paper and lumber mills it serves are older facilities with poor highway access and no potential for balancing traffic. Despite numerous attempts to solicit or coordinate backhauls, boxcars almost invariably return empty. The container is cheaper than the trailer, and may attract some traffic that piggyback cannot. But even the most ardent supporter must question whether container economics can survive the boxcar environment.

The end may come for the boxcar when the present boxcar fleet wears out. It is generally conceded the return on boxcar traffic is insufficient to justify fleet replacement. The newest boxcars are approaching their first decade of service, and with a nominal lifespan of 20 years are likely to last out the century.

Many of the plants and distribution centers that use boxcars are aging too, and new facilities rarely include rail trackage. As industry after industry is forced to reinvest and reexamine the cost of inventory, production runs and shipment sizes drop, and the demand for faster transit rises. Many older facilities are on low-density branchlines, where the economics of rail service itself are marginal. As the facilities and branchlines are retired, the boxcars that serve them are likely to be retired too.

Lumber traffic is likely to be a prime near-term target for intermodal marketers. The container is better suited than the trailer for stockpiling at distribution centers, and its lower overall costs give it a better chance of penetrating the price-sensitive lumber market. The marketing efforts, however, are likely to be aimed more at truckload competition than at boxcars – new lumber mills and distribution centers are often built without boxcar access, leaving rail with only the intermodal option.

Boxcars to boxes? Yes, and some in the very near future. The auto parts manufacturers are switching from specialized boxcars to trailers, containers, and Road-Railers®. The general purpose plain and equipped boxcar fleet, however, is deeply imbedded in the industries it serves. Until the boxcar fleet wears out or those industries change, boxcar traffic will remain a hard sell for domestic containers.

The Truck Question

By cutting costs to the bone and accepting painfully slim profit margins, piggyback carriers have managed to hold a 10-15% share of all surface freight movements over 500 miles. Although the railroads have reason to be proud of achieving that much in a very tough market, a 10-15% market share cannot be considered successful competition with long-haul trucks. Moreover, intermodal market penetration has been negligible in hauls under 500 miles, and such shorter hauls account for most intercity freight.

The doublestacked container is the most cost-efficient long-haul intermodal competitor that has yet emerged. Railroads and third parties have had some limited success in attracting the most price-sensitive truck customers. But a cost-efficient technology by itself is not enough. Intermodal has long had a cost advantage over trucks in the longest hauls, and shipper surveys have consistently found that the piggyback cost advantage is recognized in the market. Unfortunately, a low-cost, low-service option attracts low-revenue, low-profit traffic.

Door-to-door service quality is the missing element in the railroads' ability to compete successfully with trucks. Market research long ago put the matter beyond doubt. Shippers and third parties consider intermodal service to be inferior by every measure – door-to-door transit time; loss and damage experience; reliability; ease of use; tracing and claims settlement; documentation; equipment quality; and responsiveness. Some shipper perceptions may exaggerate the problems – only about half the potential long-haul intermodal customers are using intermodal at all, and current services suffer a negative "halo" effect from the lower quality piggyback services offered in the past.

The service message is preached at every industry gathering, and a few carriers and major third parties are making a serious effort to meet the service challenge. API, CSLI, and BNA have all been established as separate business units from their associated carrier to give them flexibility and single-minded management attention. Norfolk Southern's Triple Crown RoadRailer® service is also run by a separate organization for many of the same reasons. Executives of these organizations have found that new sales and marketing organizations are needed. The information systems used by the parent carriers to track and bill carload freight are often ineffective in the intermodal field, and the intermodal business units are calling for changes or building their own, parallel systems.

The goal is to provide "seamless" and "transparent" door-to-door service with a single customer contact and a single freight bill – which is exactly what a long-haul trucker provides. For many years, rail intermodal customers found they had to help manage the railroad movement by arranging drayage, calling for tracing, calling for trailer availability, and paying multiple freight bills. The actual shipper had the choice of doing that himself, or paying a third party to do it. In either case, the railroad has to charge a lower price to compensate, and cannot attract service-sensitive traffic at all.

The domestic container by itself cannot compete with long-haul trucks, but perhaps one or more of the emerging doublestack service companies can. Until the railroads or the intermodal business units can provide a door-to-door service shippers are willing to pay more for, they will have to settle for what they have.

Intermodal Equipment Leasing

As the intermodal markets continue to grow, supply of equipment has become a major preoccupation of carriers and shippers. In this regard the equipment leasing industry has been increasingly responsive to the needs of carriers, although the approach has varied depending on equipment type. The intermodal railcar leasing industry for example, is essentially dominated by a single firm, the Trailer Train Company. In sharp contrast, the structure of the container leasing industry is known for its intense competition and a "boom-bust" character as far as profits are concerned.

Although Trailer Train's total fleet of over 100,000 cars includes various rail equipment types, (boxcars, autoracks, lumber cars, etc.) its principle source of revenue is from intermodal operations (51.2% in 1987) and its fleet of some 44,000 trailer and/or container carrying flatcars. In recent years, the company has begun to acquire more specialized intermodal cars. In 1987, for example, Trailer Train purchased $89 million worth of third-generation equipment, including 1,585 doublestack wells (317 cars), 765 single-stack container platforms (153 cars) and 345 single platform cars for carrying trailers.

Cars are also being retired in greater numbers than Trailer Train adds them. However, while the typical units going out of service are capable of carrying only two trailers or containers, the new equipment types have considerably increased capacity. Doublestack cars, for example, consisting of five platforms, are capable of carrying 10 containers, each 40 feet or longer. Likewise, a spine car can carry five containers up to 48-feet in length. Despite the overall reduction in fleet size on a total car basis, therefore, the cargo carrying capacity of Trailer Train's fleet is growing.

Trailer Train continues to research new railcar types and a considerable portion of the research effort the company has undertaken over the past several years has been in the intermodal area. Among the concepts Trailer Train has experimented with and implemented are carless technologies, (e.g., RoadRailer®), doublestack cars with 125-ton instead of the conventional 100-ton trucks, and innovative ways of coupling conventional 89-foot flatcars to accommodate 53-foot containers and trailers.

The significant advantages Trailer Train has offered the intermodal rail carriers may be dwindling, however. Trailer Train operates pursuant to a pooling agreement entered into by participant railroads under authority granted by the Interstate Commerce Commission. With all its outstanding capital stock owned by US railroads, the company's sole function was to operate a pool of railcars for its owners. At the time Trailer Train was granted this antitrust immunity, however, the railroad industry was itself highly regulated. As an industry, railroading was also barely profitable, and Trailer Train's position that its equipment pooling operations could save millions of dollars by increasing utilization made sense.

Since the Staggers Act, however, and the increasing awareness among railroads that the non-competitive regulated environment is a thing of the past, the unique Trailer Train arrangement has been constantly under review. Pressure from various parties, most notably an equipment manufacturer concerned that Trailer Train's position in the market represented a purchasing monopoly, encouraged the Justice Department to petition the ICC to review the company's application to renew the arrangement for a further 15 years. In February 1989, the ICC voted to continue Trailer Train's immunity for five years, but placed restrictions on the future assignment of Trailer Train cars to specific railroads. It remains to be seen what effect this will ultimately have on intermodal railcar leasing.

In the container and chassis leasing field, change has also been taking place, albeit from a different perspective than that encountered by Trailer Train. In an industry traditionally characterized by high risk, the recession of the early part of this decade caused many container and hassis lessors to begin doubting the long-term viability of their business. It was an era dubiously remembered for teamship line bankruptcies, pamphlets analyzing the so-alled "lease-buy decision," low utilization and a circum-tance which can only be described as a protracted war etween container lessors and lessees over equipment naintenance and repair standards. These are the events bservers most often recall of the period leading up to nd immediately after 1983, a year that must rate as one f the worst years the container industry has yet uffered.

As the industry entered the last decade of the 20th entury, the outlook was remarkably different. 1988 was banner year for the business, and 1989 looked as hough it would be too. A sustained period of demand, luring which fleet utilization figures have remained in the 0% and higher range for many companies, has made the ast two years ones of great profitability. And along with igh utilization has come a reduction in many of the roblems container lessors have experienced in the past. Relations with the steamship lines and depots have nproved considerably, for example. But most signifi-antly, leasing companies are far leaner, more streamlined nd more efficient organizations than they were five years go.

Of course, the pessimists have begun predicting the next downturn. But there is little to indicate the balloon s about to burst. On the contrary, many container lessors ppear to believe the industry can remain buoyant. Nevertheless, the prospect of continued abundance has o far not inspired the traditional response – enormous sset purchases and fleet expansion in dry freight ontainers. Lessors have become wary. Probably the nost conspicuous aspect of the present period of prosperity is the conservatism of the major container lessors with regard to equipment acquisition.

Instead, managers – particularly at the privately held leasing companies – are wondering what else they might do with their money. And here the transportation industry continues to present several opportunities.

Looking specifically at the business of the two largest companies, for example, while Genstar appears content to remain a container lessor, Itel has repeatedly announced its intention to become a major league player in the intermodal transportation and distribution business. There is no denying the company is active. To date Itel Transportation Services Group has made partial or complete stock purchases in American President Companies, Santa Fe Southern Pacific Corporation, Leaseway Transportation Corporation, Pullman Leasing and at least 5 short line railroads. This wide transportation portfolio puts Itel in sharp contrast strategically to Genstar, and for that matter, most of the other container leasing firms. Only Sea Containers and Transamerica Interway have comparably diverse holdings.

In a more general sense, while the expansion of intermodalism in the US has slowed, there still remains an environment in which container lessors have been able to create new products. Significant in this regard has been the slow but real growth in the market for 45-foot and 48-foot containers. The problem for intermodal carriers and lessors however, is the ongoing international debate about what the standard dimensions of the so-called future "wide body" container ought to be. As increasing numbers of carriers begin using the larger containers, the efforts of TC/104 Working Group 4 of the International Standards Organization (ISO) to develop consensus on this issue have reached a critical point.

The desire to reach agreement on a standard for future designs of container equipment has been voiced on both sides of the Atlantic, largely, perhaps, as a response to the non-standard approach being taken by individual commercial concerns. With domestic containerization at long last poised to fulfill the promise of more than a decade, increasing numbers of non-ISO units are finding their way on to the railroads and highways. Meanwhile, the utility of containers which conform to ISO dimensions is also being threatened by the development of a rail transportation system in Europe based on the "swap-body" unit. ISO experts and commercial interests alike are suddenly anxious to standardize matters before they get out of hand.

In the Far East, the prevailing view may be one of desperation. For countries that have only recently allowed 40-foot containers at all, the prospects for widespread use of containers that exceed the present ISO maximum appear bleak. Nevertheless, even the Japanese have recognized that to participate in the standards process, however reluctantly, at least provides an opportunity to affect the direction of the seemingly inexorable march toward bigger boxes.

Still, skepticism appears to reign. As a representative from APL indicated at the joint Institute of International Container Lessors (IICL)/Institute of Intermodal Repairers (IIR)/Steamship Operators Intermodal Committee (SOIC) Container Operations '89 conference held in San Francisco in February 1989, it may be 10 years before any real agreement can be reached on larger box sizes. Whatever direction the international standards process may take, however, so far it has not stopped various lessors from investing in 45-foot and 48-foot equipment, mostly to supply the railroads. XTRA Corporation has been particularly active in this field.

Apart from the new size containers, chassis pools, both at inland rail terminals and now increasingly at ocean port terminal locations, have also presented major opportunities for lessors. Chassis pools are an interesting indicator of the future of leasing organizations not because of the equipment involved but because lessors have found that logistics management skills are a marketable commodity. For example, while there would be little to stop a marine terminal from purchasing its own chassis to fund a pool, significantly, in most cases terminal operators have sought out the services of leasing companies.

Specialized equipment continues to be attractive to container lessors as an alternative area of expansion which complements the core dry freight business. Refrigerated containers and tank containers, both of which will be significant in the intermodal systems of the future, seem to be flourishing, the latter despite an ongoing battle lessors are having with the United States Department of Transportation over proposed new rules for hazardous materials transportation. In these and other niche markets, the container equipment lessor can expect to find a profitable investment opportunity.

But individual lessors' various responses to overall growth in transportation markets, although significant, are not by themselves distinguishing characteristics of the present day leasing industry, compared with its counterpart five years ago. What identifiable characteristics differentiate today's container lessors?

One of the most remarkable developments of the

past few years has been the so-called "rationalization" of the industry. This has taken place in two ways: from a corporate standpoint, and in relation to the overall utilization of the world's fleet.

Although the business community in general has expressed doubts about the long-term effects of the merger and acquisition "mania" which has swept the United States corporate world over the past three years, in the container leasing sector the response has been dramatically different. Despite the fact that almost 50% of the world's leased containers are now controlled by just two companies, no one has complained about the impact on free-market competition. Quite the reverse; such mergers have been proclaimed a good thing for the industry, even a necessity for its survival. Thus it may have been with some relief that competitors watched Genstar conclude its acquisition of the Gelco CTI fleet early in 1988. Similarly, few bemoaned the fate of the industry when Itel purchased the XTRA and Flexi-Van marine container fleets.

The concept of the "Seven Sisters" is forever a thing of the past. For one thing, of the original market leaders, Gelco CTI, Sea Containers, Transamerica Container Leasing, Interpool, Itel, Flexi-Van and XTRA, one company no longer exists and two have essentially exited the marine container leasing business. Of the seven, only Sea Containers and Transamerica Container Leasing are left unchanged, although the latter, by assuming the management of NIC Leasing, was among the first firms to use a merger as a means of improving its market position.

But second, the distinction between the largest companies and the so called "second generation" lessors has been eroded. Firms such as Trans Ocean Leasing and

Textainer have also engineered takeovers of smaller fleets. And, although the size of these companies, along with Triton Container, Intermodal Equipment Associates, UK-based Tiphook Container Rental and the German company CLOU Containers, remains smaller than Itel, Genstar, Sea Containers and Transamerica Container Leasing, there is no appreciable difference in the range or scope of the business these firms are conducting in international dry freight container leasing.

Has the rationalization process among the largest companies ended? Some would say no. Interpool has been the subject of several takeover rumors and, early in 1989, Transamerica Container Leasing acquired several thousand high cube containers from the company, further depleting the company's revenue earning abilities. Meanwhile, no one believes Itel's appetite has been satiated, and rumors of the eventual emergence of a 1,000,000 TEU company were being heard with increasing frequency.

Rationalization has not only taken place at the corporate level. Increasingly, container leasing companies have sought to acquire or gain management control of assets owned by other, non-lessor corporations. TOL, for example, was particularly active in the wake of the bankruptcy of United States Lines, and has recently taken over management of Showa Line's container and chassis fleets.

The willingness to build fleet size with used assets is a relatively new phenomenon and is explained by a number of factors. There is the fact, for example, that used containers, of the right kind, are available in sufficient numbers to make acquisition deals worthwhile. Previously, although a few deals came around from time to time, nothing equaling the opportunities afforded by the failure of US Lines had existed.

Second, the rising price of new containers in the Far East has provided container lessors with an incentive to find alternative sources of equipment. With manufacturers quotes approaching $3,000 for delivery of 20-foot containers, lessors have literally been forced into responsible purchasing strategies. But, apart from price, there may be a growing recognition among leasing strategists that, ultimately, the success of their business is and will always remain a function of the total number of usable containers situated around the world. This is a far cry from the golden age of container purchasing during which, it seems, lessors did not seem to notice or care that, on a global scale, simply too many pieces of equipment were being acquired. At any rate, acquisition of existing assets not only increases individual fleet sizes, but avoids new equipment coming onto the market.

The trend toward "asset rationalization" has another important aspect – an organized approach to retiring equipment after it has outlived its maritime usefulness. With the used container market much more clearly defined than it was five years ago, most of the larger leasing companies have developed the contacts and expertise necessary to allow them to realize good values selling to the wholesale markets. Itel, for instance, is moving into the used market in a big way with Instant Space, and others are even looking at retail markets. Almost all the major lessors have recognized that containers have a tremendous after-market value and have established a means of cashing in. And the effect this is having on the leasing business is significant. As the after market expands and used container values in many locations increase, lessors are finding the decision to retire equipment easier to make.

The process of corporate and asset rationalization has undoubtedly resulted in an industry better equipped to manage both its personnel resources and its equipment. Arguably, from an overall industry perspective, the fact that upward of one million TEUs are now under the control of two firms is simply more efficient than the way the same number of containers were managed five years ago. Centralization has resulted in better control, while the reduction of personnel overhead (on a per unit basis) and the increased use of automated systems has and will further bring the cost of doing business down.

Perhaps as a measure of the leasing industry's health, its trade association, the Institute of International Container Lessors has emerged from a period of uncertainty and can now claim to be a truly representative organization. One of the IICL's notable achievements has been its vigorous pursuit of objective engineering knowledge of the physical characteristics of container equipment, especially when damaged. And even the most jaded critic would be hard pressed not to admit that IICL's container testing program provides valuable data. For many the testing program rates as one of the association's major triumphs.

One of the most significant developments the industry is likely to see over the next few years is the introduction of electronic data interchange for collecting and distributing information about lease transactions. Genstar has implemented a system and now receives data electronically from many of its depots. Other lessors, anxious to find a way to reduce transaction costs as well as the volume of paper the industry produces, are expected to follow Genstar's lead, and also to expand the capabilities of any system to include steamship lines, railroads, truckers and other parties that get involved in container movements. Like other industries, the possibility of one or more public data networks being developed for container lessors and their trading partners has become a reality with the rapid advance of EDI technology. In a few years, EDI could revolutionize the way data moves and how data are used to control logistic activity and the repair and maintenance process.

One other factor is significant in judging the status of the leasing industry. On the legal front, the leasing industry has yet to establish a comfortable status within international admiralty law. At issue is the right of lessors to seize vessels owned or operated by companies that fail to pay per diem rental invoices. Various courts in the US and Europe have ruled differently on cases involving vessel seizure by a lessor. But of some significance might be a recent ruling by the United Kingdom House of Lords involving the seizure, by Tiphook Container Rental, of a ship operated by Nigerian Shipping Line. The House of Lords denied Tiphook's right to seize the *River Rima*, citing the fact that lease contracts covering the containers in question did not specify the vessel to which the equipment had been furnished.

Few lease agreements ever specify the vessels on which containers will or might be loaded, nor, are they ever likely to. Judgments such as that handed down by the House of Lords therefore present an ongoing and vexing problem for container lessors.

The intermodal revolution has clearly given equipment lessors something to think about. For Trailer Train, it looks as though business conditions will be more competitive following the ICC decision. For container lessors, the intermodal revolution presents the challenge of new equipment risks and different markets with different customers.

Information Technologies

In an industrial society the strategic resource is capital. In our post-industrial society, the strategic resource has become information. However, the amount of information generated has become too large to handle, necessitating a shift away from supply and toward selection. Information technology has to bring order to the chaos of "information pollution" and it must add value to data that would otherwise be useless.

In the field of intermodal transportation, the expansion of business in recent years has placed a premium on the use of advanced information technologies. Intermodal transportation is fast reaching the point where information management has become a key ingredient of success. More importantly, reliance on computers and electronic data communication is likely to increase several-fold over the next few years, as transportation services become more complex and customer sensitive.

Two technologies in particular, Electronic Data Interchange (EDI) and Automatic Equipment Identification (AEI), promise to change the way business is conducted in the transportation sector, and specifically in the intermodal business.

Electronic Data Interchange

EDI is a tool that can add value to data. It is usually

defined as the direct computer-to-computer exchange of standard business forms. Its benefits have been summed up as providing a system in which data is entered only once, information is transferred simultaneously to all parties, standardized documents and message formats are electronically provided and information exchange and documentation costs are significantly reduced.

The extent to which EDI has and will continue to effect intermodalism has been the subject of more seminars, newspaper reports and journal articles than perhaps any other single development in international transportation over the past two years. EDI is big news in many industries, but no more so than in transportation, where the sheer number of duplicated information gathering and manual paper functions has reached a stifling level. Railroads, steamship lines, truckers and even government agencies have recognized the need to eliminate paper and to automate the transmission of standard business documents.

Although EDI is not a complex technology as such, what it facilitates is nothing short of revolutionary in data processing terms. It involves the interchange of business data between computers and provides a system whereby different and often incompatible software and hardware systems can be linked over huge geographical distances. EDI involves the replacement of paper documents, and the common methods of transferring those documents from company to company, such as facsimile and mail, with the electronic communication of information. Using structured electronic messages, data about business transactions can be transferred directly from one computer to another.

EDI uses common electronic document formats. In

the US, TDCC – The Electronic Data Interchange Association – has been one of the most influential organizations dealing with the design of electronic transportation documents. TDCC standards are approved by the American National Standards Institute (ANSI) X.12 Committee which has control over the design of EDI documents used in a broad spectrum of industries. Internationally, the general standard for electronic data interchange will in the future be the United Nations sanctioned EDI for Administration, Commerce and Transport (EDIFACT) design. EDIFACT is really a system of rules for designing documents and is, for example, the basis for the International Freight Transportation Message (IFTM) and for the new ISO-designed Container Equipment Data Exchange (CEDEX) documents being used on the Control Data Redinet third-party global network.

Another essential ingredient of standardized EDI is the use of a third party "mailbox" system, or clearinghouse for EDI messages. For example, EDI has been in use in the railroad industry for several years. In fact the AAR operates a third-party network, Railinc (one of the oldest EDI systems), which provides EDI services to the rail industry. Other major network companies competing for part of the intermodal market include McDonnell Douglas, Control Data Corporation, IBM, General Electric Information Services (GEIS), Kleinschmidt and Ordernet.

Historically railroads have been aggressive about EDI implementation. As Figure 6-2 shows, Railinc transmission volumes have been growing at a significant rate since early in the '80's. Much of this volume is bill of lading information, electronically transmitted using Railinc's EDI mailboxes, as opposed to using traditional

240

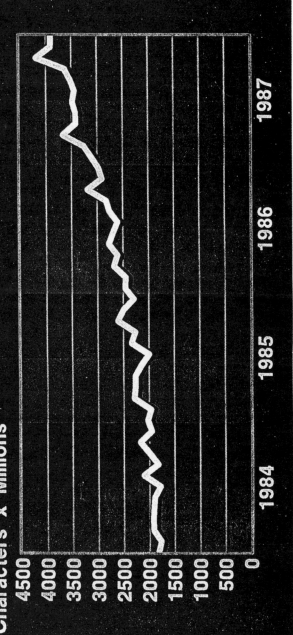

NETWORK MONTHLY EDI TRAFFIC

Characters x Millions

4500
4000
3500
3000
2500
2000
1500
1000
500
0

1984   1985   1986   1987

Growth of EDI for railroad-related purposes is evident in this graph of transmissions handled by Railinc over a four year period.

Figure 6-2   From April 1988 Intermodal Age.

manual paper systems. When a shipper's agent wants to send a bill of lading for an intermodal shipment to the railroad carrier, he or she creates and sends the document from a computer keyboard. Transmissions such as these take about one minute to accomplish, compared to about 30 minutes for paper.

Bills of lading are used in the marine sector in the same way as in the railroad business, and steamship lines have also been quick to implement ways of sending electronic versions of these types of documents. Ocean carriers do not, however, have the luxury of a third-party network system tailored exclusively to their needs. Steamship lines are using a variety of interconnected networks or in some cases, direct links with their customers or agents, in order to make the necessary connections. Lines such as Sea-Land Services, American President Lines, Trans Freight Lines, Hapag Lloyd and Maersk Lines are heavily involved in EDI implementation. Other ocean carriers are sure to follow suit as the benefits of the technology are more clearly identified.

Also active in EDI are the ports, the US Customs Service and other federal agencies. The Automated Cargo Expediting System (ACES) run by the Port of New York/New Jersey provides an example of a port system. There are indications of a growing desire among many port operators and officials to standardize information that ports receive and dispense from steamship lines and their customers.

Among the intermodal carriers, draymen have been slowest to implement EDI technology. This is understandable because draymen rarely have primary responsibility for intermodal shipments and much of the data presently being transmitted via EDI is of little concern to them.

This may change however, as new EDI products come on the market.

One approach, for example, is an international EDI system for equipment tracking. While most EDI implementation has concentrated on cargo-related documents such as bills of lading, ship manifests, etc., Control Data Redinet, in cooperation with Oakland-based Cedex, Inc., now offers a global EDI system for use by carriers, depot and terminal operators, leasing companies and draymen. Using Cedex software and the Redinet network, railroads and steamship lines can get container and chassis on- and off-lease, repair and maintenance and other inventory control and tracking information for their leasing company suppliers and depots.

There is little doubt that EDI will continue to make major inroads in the intermodal transportation business, both domestically and internationally. Just what will result from the widespread adoption of EDI techniques remains to be seen, however. While the technology promises enormous efficiencies, the cost of implementation still leaves many in doubt. Most importantly, to be really effective, EDI requires the commitment of entire industries and, specifically, of the major players within those industries. Without trading partner cooperation, the realization of EDI's benefits will be slow, and in a time- and price-sensitive business like intermodalism, the respective abilities of companies willing to make EDI work will represent a significant factor in product differentiation in the future.

Automatic Equipment Identification

Despite the tremendous advances made during recent years in information technology, pertinent data on each container entering or leaving through most intermodal terminal gates is still recorded manually. This time consuming, labor intensive process, which is prone to mistakes, has yet to be fully automated. But at last there seems to be a remedy. Radio Frequency Identification (RFID) technology has been shown to be capable of meeting the demanding requirements for an AEI system, and doing it quite well.

Not only can RFID equipment record data automatically, it has the capability of doing it much more quickly, reliably and accurately than operators who are inputting information through computer terminals. In fact, test results indicate that RFID equipment has a reading accuracy greater than 99.9% – virtually an error-free performance. Thus, the potential benefits to be gained from an RFID-based AEI system, in terms of time and money savings, as well as improved overall efficiency, are dramatic. Unlike the earlier (and often unreliable) railroad automatic car identification systems that utilized optical scanners to read labels on railcars, RFID uses bi-directional radio signals as its communications medium.

A typical RFID system has three primary components – a programmed identification transponder or "tag," an antenna, and a transmitter/reader. The tag is attached to the equipment to be tracked. It operates on a specific frequency, transmitting its distinctive "signature" or data stream in response to an interrogation by the transmitter/reader. The antenna picks up the signal and the reader then demodulates, decodes and validates the signal for transmission to a host computer.

The tags can be either "active" or "passive." An active tag has a built-in battery, whereas a passive tag has o internal power source. Active tags are less affected by positioning, have better electronic noise immunity and have a longer range than passive tags; however, they are more expensive and, because of the battery, do not have an indefinite life span.

Some RFID systems provide a "write" capability that allows the system to add information to the tag as it passes the transmitter/reader. This feature can be used to create a portable data base that includes additional information about a container such as its consignee, its destination or the presence of hazardous cargo.

Two of the major US suppliers of RFID equipment for the transportation industry are General Railway Signal Co. of Rochester, N.Y., and the Amtech Corporation of Dallas, Texas.

The GRS RFID system, known as "Identifier," uses a frequency doubling technique in which a signal is transmitted to the tag at 906MHz and returned from the tag at 1812 MHz. All Identifier tags are the passive type with permanently fixed codes and a maximum operating range of 30 feet.

The Amtech RFID system uses a modulated back-scatter technique in which the transmitted frequency to the tag and the reflected frequency from the tag are the same. Amtech offers both a passive tag that operates at 915MHz with a maximum range of 60 feet and an active tag that operates at both 915MHz (maximum range of 250 feet) and 2.45GHz (maximum range of 180 feet). Union Switch & Signal of Pittsburgh, Pa. uses Amtech components in its "Shadow" electronic identification system.

Through several test programs conducted in cooperation with steamship lines and the US government, both AEI suppliers have successfully demonstrated the operational capabilities of their RFID systems under actual intermodal operating conditions. These tests, along with others conducted on railroads (including one test conducted on the French TGV train in which tags were read at speeds up to 180 mph), clearly pointed out that RFID can work in the rugged and demanding maritime, rail and highway environments that affect intermodal transportation.

In a test program conducted for the Matson Navigation Co. at its Oakland, CA terminal, 1,000 GRS Identifier tags were attached to container chassis and motor generator sets, and three readers were installed at the terminal gates to identify the equipment pieces as they entered and left the terminal. Although containers were not used in these tests, Matson was provided with a convincing demonstration of what the technology was capable of doing.

Amtech's RFID equipment was used in a series of tests conducted in 1987 for American President Companies, Sea-Land Services and the US Department of Defense. In the APC tests readers were placed at gates and on various cranes and container handling equipment to track movements of containers in and around APC's Oakland terminal. A mobile inventory vehicle (a truck instrumented with a reader) was also used for automatic inventory of containers and chassis in the yard.

For the Sea-Land tests, an Amtech system was installed in the steamship line's Anchorage, Alaska yard. Four reading stations at the yard gate were instrumented to test the worldwide capability of the Amtech system. The Department of Defense tested an Amtech system for tracking US Army supply containers shipped from Oakland to Okinawa.

The obstacles standing in the way of universal adoption of automatic container identification systems seem more institutional then technological. Perhaps the single most important issue facing carriers who are eager to install AEI systems is the lack of an established international standard. Without such an accepted standard on the books, the risk of selecting a given supplier's AEI equipment are high, since no carrier wants to have an AEI system that is not compatible with the rest of the world's. This issue is probably one of the foremost concerns many carriers have about implementing AEI systems for their containers.

Because of this concern, the Cargo Handling Cooperative Program (CHCP), whose membership includes the US flag steamship lines of American President Lines, Sea-Land and Matson Navigation and the US Maritime Administration, decided to address the standardization issue. CHCP developed a draft AEI standard in 1986 that was submitted for further evaluation to Working Group 3 (Freight Containers – Coding & marking) of ISO Technical Committee 104. After making some revisions to CHCP's efforts, WG 3, in turn, prepared an ISO draft standard. This draft AEI standard, which was bassed on RFID technology, was circulated for review by ISO membership.

Major elements of the draft standard included the following recommended specifications:

- A solid state transponder that operates in the 888-889 MHz, 902-928 MHz, and 2.4-2.5 GHz bands.

- A 19 character modified ASCII six-bit transponder code to describe the data on a container's type, its alphanumberic ID number and its tare weight, length and height.

- The location of the transponder on a container to be on the forward right wall at the front edge adjacent to the roof. (For containers longer than 40 feet the transponder location is to be just aft of the 40-foot corner casting position.)

The recommended specifications also dealt with signal strength and other technical details. It is anticipated that a final standard could be ratified by ISO at any time.

APC, apparently pleased with the test results of the Amtech RFID equipment and, perhaps, anticipating ISO's adoption of the proposed standards, began in 1989 to phase in an AEI system based on Amtech's RFID technology. APC's system, which represents the first operational application of RFID in the container transportation industry, involves the installation of over 20,000 transponders on APC equipment – 10,500 on containers, 9,700 on chassis, 250 on trucks and 240 on double-stack cars. Prior to installation, each tag is programmed with its respective piece of equipment's identification.

AIE transmitter/readers and associated computers were initially to be installed at APC's West Coast port facilities in Seattle and Los Angeles (San Pedro), as well as at Union Pacific Railroad facilities in Seattle, Portland and Los Angeles. The APC system conforms to the standards drafted by the CHCP. The initial phase-in of APC's AEI system was scheduled for completion in mid-1989. If successful, the company said it will consider

Figure 6-3 One of the first transponders installed on an APL 45-foot container passes by an AEI reader. Courtesy American President Companies

expanding the use of AEI to all major ports and rail terminals and installing tags on additional equipment as necessary.

RFID clearly offers an inexpensive, highly reliable means of identifying a container as it passes locations equipped with transmitter/readers. However, as capable as it is, because of the very limited range of the transponders, RFID does not offer a means of continuously tracking containers as they move throughout their journeys. Other, more sophisticated electronic technologies, such as the Advanced Railway Electronic System (ARES) and the Radio Determination Satellite Service (RDSS), do offer that possibility.

Both ARES and RDSS solve the same two-part problem – determining the geographical position of the equipment (e.g., container, railcar, truck) and then transmitting that position data back to a central location, quite often a considerable distance away.

ARES-equipped locomotives receive position data from Navstar Global Positioning System satellites, as well as in-track RFID transponders. Strategically placed in-track transponders, along with an on-board transmitter/reader, are needed to determine the exact track on which a train is operating when it is in multiple track areas, since satellite positioning is not precise enough to do that. This position data is processed by an on-board computer, then transmitted via VHF radio to a distant control center. ARES, which was developed by Rockwell International, has been tested by the Burlington Northern Railroad on its unit ore trains operating in the Iron Range of northern Minnesota.

RDSS uses satellites, radio and computers in a

somewhat different fashion to solve the same problem. An onboard receiver picks up signals from the US government-operated Loran C radio navigation system which provides an electronic grid used by both ships and aircraft to determine position. These position coordinates are then transmitted to a satellite which, in turn, retransmits them to the Geostar Corporation receiver in Washington, D.C. From there, the position data is sent via telephone to a central computer where it can be distributed to subscribers of the service. Frederick Transport, a Canadian-based trucking company, began installing RDSS equipment on its US fleet of 220 trucks in 1988.

Theoretically, both ARES and RDSS offer the potential for continuously tracking containers within the United States. However, since the number of freight containers in the world is estimated to be five million, the cost of equipping all of them with the sophisticated electronic packages needed for either system makes the idea of continuously tracking individual containers cost-prohibitive at this time. For the immediate future, it looks as if carriers will have to be satisfied with the capability of automatically identifying containers as they pass selected locations. But even that represents a vast improvement over what they have now.

Damage, Liability and Claims

Damage

Today's intermodal shippers have much less to worry about when it comes to loss and damage than they did in the past. New vehicle and load restraint technologies, backed up by better operating practices, have brought the

251

ride quality and security of the rail portion of intermodal moves up to or above the high levels experienced during the motor carrier portion of the moves.

Nevertheless, improperly or inadequately stowed cargo in containers or piggyback trailers can still cause problems. Lading that has been incorrectly loaded or secured can burst through the ends of trailers or containers, even under normal conditions encountered during transit. A sideways lading shift in a piggyback trailer can cause it to lean excessively and, in some cases, actually fall off the flatcar, possibly leading to a derailment. At the very least, once it is discovered, a flatcar that has a leaning trailer or a trailer (or container) with distressed doors must be set out, causing an unnecessary delay enroute. When at sea, the contents of damaged containers may end up going overboard.

The unexpected costs, both direct and indirect, resulting from mishaps in which cargo has shifted can be staggering. Thousands of dollars worth of damage to goods, loss of sales and good will, disruption to service, lawsuits, injuries or even deaths, all can occur if the shipper has failed to take a little extra time or money to secure the goods adequately while loading a container or trailer. Quite often the shipper using the latest technology in load restraints need only invest a few minutes and several hundred dollars to insure against potentially catastrophic losses.

This is not to say that intermodal shipping is inherently dangerous or risky. On the contrary, containers and piggyback trailers significantly help to minimize exposure of goods to damage by eliminating unnecessary rehandling and providing a secure, dry environment. Indeed, the intermodal shipment record speaks for itself.

"The vast majority of all intermodal shipments move damage-free," reported a damage prevention expert for the Association of American Railroads. "Of course, the small percent incurring damage are the ones you hear about."

Detailed information on approved loading methods for intermodal cargo is provided in AAR Circular 43-A, revised in 1989. In addition to this document, most of the major railroads publish their own intermodal loading manuals for their customers. For the marine environment, the Maritime Administration publishes a book titled *A Shipper's Guide to Stowage of Cargo in Marine Container.* There is no shortage of material available describing how goods should be loaded and secured for the intermodal environment.

The AAR has an ongoing program to perform research on new intermodal loading and securement methods using its modern facilities located at the Transportation Test Center in Pueblo, Colo. One of these facilities is the Vibration Test Unit (VTU), a full-scale rail environment simulator that significantly reduces the amount of time and testing required to evaluate new securement systems. Having the VTU has greatly enhanced the AAR's testing capability at Pueblo. In 1983 there were just eight intermodal loading and securement methods published by the AAR damage prevention group, but by 1989 there were 27. In 1987 and 1988 alone, the AAR evaluated 67 intermodal systems.

Intermodal shippers have to be prepared to deal with as many as three different transportation environments – rail, highway and marine – each with its own unique conditions. Regardless of the particular mode, there are two types of forces exerted on goods in transport: shock (resulting from abrupt changes in acceleration and direction) and vibration (resulting from continuous oscillations), These forces can act along any of the three axes of the transporting vehicle – vertical, longitudinal and lateral. Whenever force levels exceed the limits of securement systems, damage to lading and equipment can occur. The intermodal shipper must be aware of the transportation environments his cargo will experience during its journey, then stow and secure it for the worst conditions.

In the rail environment, longitudinal shock, usually associated with car coupling (switching) operations, is generally the most severe force encountered. Coupling is done in two ways, either by shoving cars together with a locomotive or by setting cars in motion, then releasing them to coast along a classification track until they are stopped by friction or another car, as is done in "hump" yards. The degree of longitudinal shock experienced by lading during coupling depends upon the type of operation and several other factors. Under some circumstances, it can be quite high. Because of the slack in conventional coupling systems, longitudinal shock forces are also produced when a train stretches (known as run-out) while starting up from a dead stop or ascending a grade or when it contracts (known as run-in) while stopping or descending a grade.

Besides the longitudinal forces experienced during typical train operations, piggyback trailers are also subjected to lateral movements, or sway, resulting from rolling motion. Although a lateral movement of up to four degrees either side of the vertical has been observed in extreme situations, usual TOFC roll angles are less than one degree. Because of its higher center of gravity and the fact that it is riding on two suspension systems (its own and the flatcar's), a TOFC trailer experiences more rolling motion than a container on a flatcar.

The much-vaunted doublestack car has helped considerably to mitigate the effects of longitudinal forces, lateral (rolling) forces and vertical vibrations experienced by traditional TOFC/COFC cargo. A doublestack unit train, with its five-platform articulated cars, has only 20% the number of couplers as an equally long conventional train, and consequently experiences much less slack action during coupling and transit. Furthermore, because the bottom containers riding on doublestack cars sit in wells, the height of the combined center of gravity of the stacked containers is actually lower than that of piggyback trailers sitting on flatcars, thus assuring greater lateral stability for stack train cargo than TOFC cargo. Also, with their reduced distance between truck centers, doublestack cars experience significantly lower vibrational forces than conventional TOFC/COFC flatcars.

Carless trains, too, provide a better ride for goods than conventional TOFC trailers. Since they have a slackless coupling system, carless trains (which so far are operated exclusively in unit trains that never see a hump yard) experience virtually no slack action. Furthermore, since there are no flatcars involved, carless technologies have a lower center of gravity, thus less sway, and one less suspension system, thus less vertical vibration, than their piggyback cousins.

In recent years, the railroads have made great strides in reducing the forces cargo experiences during its time on the rails. In addition to introducing new equipment such as doublestacks and carless technologies, railroads have taken several other important steps to improve the ride for their intermodal traffic. The replacement of jointed rail with continuous welded rail helps to reduce vertical vibrations induced by rail joints. Exposure to severe longitudinal shock from coupling has been greatly minimized by operating intermodal cars in unit trains. In fact, humping of doublestack cars is not ever permitted.

Compared to the rail environment, vertical vibration is generally considered more severe in the highway environment. A continuous vertical vibration input known as a forcing function is produced while the truck and trailer tires are in contact with the roadway surface. Under certain circumstances, when the forcing frequency is the same as the natural frequency of the suspension system, amplification of the forces can occur and "bogie bounce" may result. If the bounce is extreme enough, lading inside the trailer (or container on a chassis) can shift. Uneven conditions on highway surfaces, such as holes or abrupt changes in pavement, can also cause vertical shocks that can be greater than those occurring to railcars.

Trucks also experience longitudinal shocks from rapid accelerations and sudden stops, such as backing into a dock. However, the magnitude of longitudinal shocks seen by trucks is usually less than that for railcars. Lateral forces on trucks are similar in strength to lateral forces on railcars.

The ocean creates the most complex and rigorous forces occurring in any of the three intermodal environments. The toughest leg of any intermodal journey can often be on the sea. Not only do the containers experience linear motions along all three of a ship's axes, they also get treated to rotational motion about all three axes. Because of the unpredictability of the sea, the number

256

and magnitude of the forces acting on containerized cargo aboard ship can far exceed those experienced during land transportation.

Often, several of these ship's motions are occurring simultaneously, producing a very complicated set of forces that act on containers and their cargo. Even one of these motions acting alone can be quite severe. For example, a roll of 45-degrees is not uncommon in heavy seas. In such conditions a container can travel through an arc 70 feet long, as often as seven to 10 times per minute.

Traditional blocking and bracing using lumber is not commonly done anymore for most intermodal cargo, particularly for traffic involved in land movements only. In part, this may be the result of a test series conducted by the AAR in 1984 to evaluate the ability of trailer doors to restrain lading. Prior to these tests AAR rules prohibited using doors as lading restraint. However, based on the conclusions of the study, the AAR updated its rules to allow the use of trailer doors as load securement under specific load parameters. With loads under 40,000 pounds, the end doors of piggyback trailers and containers are adequate restraint, provided the lading encompasses at least 60% of the doorway area and it is loaded tightly.

Another reason for the infrequent use of blocking and bracing for intermodal traffic is the availability of alternative AAR-approved load restraint methods that are both cheaper and faster to install. These systems, developed and sold by several manufacturers, use instant-bonding straps, steel pallet restraints, or inflatable dunnage bags to prevent loads from shifting within the trailer or container. Because these commercially available load restraint devices effectively eliminate the need for traditional blocking and bracking, many shippers prefer to use them.

Liability and Claims

Certainly one of the best ways of avoiding damage claims altogether is through the proper stowage of cargo in the first place. But, despite even the best efforts of shippers and carriers alike, damage to goods still occurs. When this does happen, the shipper must file a claim to recover the losses, thus raising the issue of liability. Under common law (codified in the 1906 Carmack Amendment and the 1915 Cummins Amendment to the Interstate Commerce Act), interstate railroads and motor carriers, as common carriers, are liable up to the full value of the cargo in the event of loss or damage, unless one or more of the following five exceptions is present:

- An act of God, e.g., a natural catastrophe such as a flood or earthquake.

- An act of public enemy, e.g., military action of a foreign government.

- An act of public authority, e.g., goods seized by law enforcement or other government officials.

- An act or omission of the shipper, e.g., improper loading of cargo.

- The inherent nature of the goods, e.g., shrinkage or spoilage.

Furthermore, shippers are not required to prove

that the carrier's negligence caused the loss or damage.

The liability of domestic water carriers is also covered under the Interstate Commerce Act. As with interstate rail and motor carriers, the domestic water carriers are liable for the full actual loss, unless they can demonstrate that the loss or damage was caused by one or more of the five exceptions listed above or by the additional exceptions of perils of the water, errors in navigation, rescue efforts and fire. Thus, domestic water carriers have a much more limited liability than their land-bound counterparts.

When it comes to liability limitations, ocean carriers have even a better deal than domestic water carriers. US ocean carriers are covered under the Carriage of Goods by Sea Act (COGSA) of 1936, the provisions of which were adapted from a 1924 treaty known as the Hague Rules. COGSA allows 17 exceptions, or "defenses," that limit the liability of ocean carriers. In addition to the exceptions covering domestic water carriers, ocean carriers, as stated in the act, are relieved of the responsibility of a loss caused by an "Act, neglect, or default of the master, mariner, pilot, or the servants of the carrier in words, if a ship's captain causes damage or loss to his ship's cargo through his own negligence or mismanagement, the carrier is not liable. Not only that, even when an ocean carrier is found to be liable, the maximum extent of its liability is only $500 per package or "customary shipping unit." Normally, the ocean bill of lading describes what is meant by package, however, in some cases an entire container has been ruled to be a package.

Because intermodal movements often involve more than one carrier, determining who is liable for lost or damaged cargo is a more complex problem than in single carrier situations. The problem is further complicated by the many different intermodal plans and options available the different types of bills of lading used, and whether or not the intermodal movements are domestic or international.

In some domestic TOFC/COFC moves, a railroad's responsibility for a loaded trailer or container is only from ramp to ramp. Since the railroads do not permit opening trailer or container doors at the ramps to inspect the cargo and how it is loaded, they quite often refuse to accept the liability for damage, claiming there is not proof that the damage occurured while the trailer or container was in their possession. When, however, a railroad's intermodal services are door-to-door, the question of the cargo's condition at the ramp becomes irrelevant, since the railroad has control of the trailer or container for its entire move. In the case of a motor carrier that issues a through bill of lading for a TOFC/COFC shipment, it usually carries the liability for damaged cargo and the railroad is relieved of the responsibility. With more and more third parties now arranging intermodal shipments the determination of liability has become even more confused.

To help eliminate the confusion for its shippers, Conrail, early in 1989, announced a program that should solve some of the problems wtih claims procedures. Conrail promises that shippers will be able to deal directly with a responsible single contact – from among a group of selected intermodal retailers (third parties) – on all claims resulting from shipments made via Conrail dedicated intermodal trains between points on its system. Such claims will be acknowledged within 30 days of receipt. A shipper with a claim will be paid or advised of ts disposition within 60 days. The standard maximum liability is $250,000 per trailer or container, although a full coverage option is available at additional cost through the intermodal retailers.

Much of the international traffic that travels in combined containership/doublestack train service moves on ocean bills of lading. Each steamship line offering these services has different policies in handling claims when the damage occurs during the inland portion of the movement. Some lines accept claims involving the inland portion, while others do not. If the location of the damage cannot be determined, ocean carriers presume that it occurred while the goods were in their possession. Usually the limit of the liability is $500 per package, as established by the Hague Rules.

Prior to deregulation, "released value rates" – in which the carrier assumes less than full value liability for the goods and the shipper pays a lower than normal tariff – were not permitted in interstate rail and highway transportation unless specifically authorized by the ICC. Consequently, before 1980, few such rates existed. However, with the passage of the Staggers Rail Act of 1980 and the Motor Carrier Act of 1980, this restriction was removed. Both railroads and motor carriers can now establish released rates without needing the approval of the ICC. This development has affected both intermodal and non-intermodal rates.

Most TOFC/COFC circulars published since Staggers automatically limit the railroad's liability. Therefore, it behooves shippers to examine very closely bills of lading, tariff circulars and other rate information published by carriers to determine the exact limits of liability assumed by carriers for given rates. It seems that released rates for TOFC/COFC services are now the norm, and shippers should be well aware of that fact.

Chapter 7

INTERMODAL FUTURE

Spurred on by the new freedoms of deregulation, the improved efficiencies of newer technologies and major shifts in world trade patterns, the intermodal revolution that swept through the freight transportation industry during the 1970s and 1980s brought with it dramatic changes in the way goods are moved, whether across the country or around the world. Yet intermodalism has only begun to demonstrate its full potential. To be sure, container ships have largely replaced break-bulk ships in the movement of non-bulk commodities by sea; but the inland movement of these goods in the US still remains largely in the hands of long-haul truckers.

The arguments favoring rail-truck transit over straight truck movement can be convincing. It has been estimated by the Association of American Railroads that a railroad can move a given quantity of freight for one-fifth the fuel, one-sixth the accidents and one-tenth of land required to carry the same load by motor carrier. Furthermore, even with less than optimal labor agreements, railroads carry seven times as much freight per employee as motor carriers. The benefits railroad intermodal offers are enormous in terms of reducing the problems of air pollution, minimizing the requirements for land usage, decreasing the consumption of fossil fuel, maximizing safety and maximizing productivity. Yet despite these important benefits, railroad intermodal, for many reasons, is still way behind over-the-road haulage in terms of the amount of goods moved.

It would seem that many barriers stand in the way of a more fully developed system of intermodal transportation in the US – labor issues, infrastructure needs, governmental policies (or the lack thereof) and the relatively low cost of fossil fuel, to name only a few. Nevertheless, progress in intermodal transportation is certain to continue now that it has proved itself to be a viable, efficient system for moving freight. New ideas and new opportunities will foster more growth. So in spite of the many obstacles facing it, the future of intermodalism remains bright.

What follows is an assessment of the key challenges for future intermodal development.

New Traffic Opportunities

With only about 4% of US intercity highway traffic moving intermodally, there are clearly immense new traffic opportunities for intermodal carriers. From the railroad point of view, intermodal transportation has always been a premium service for high-rated commodities such as mail, perishables and consumer goods. As explained in Chapter 5, the boxcar remains the current and near-term choice for numerous commodities, such as lumber, with lower values or specialized equipment needs. There are many other commodities, such as household goods, that rarely move by rail at all, because neither intermodal nor carload services have been able to compete with trucks.

From the ocean carriers' point of view, nearly everything that can fit in a container is moved in a container, including liquids, bulks and even livestock. Where containers are not used, it is either because small ports do not have adequate equipment, or because some other advanced handling method (such as roll-on/roll-off) has proven superior.

Will domestic intermodal service be able to compete for new commodities? The answer is yes. While few observers are prepared to argue that intermodal transportation will dominate domestic intercity freight, efforts are underway to attract new commodities ranging from household goods to household garbage, and the initial results from some of these experiments have been encouraging.

For example, household goods movement is the target of some recent new intermodal marketing efforts. This traffic is a distinct specialty, even within the motor carrier industry, involving different companies, equipment, and regulations. If nothing else, the poor loss-and-damage reputation of past piggyback services would have kept household goods off the rails indefinitely. Improvements in intermodal operations and equipment, especially the use of articulated piggyback or doublestack cars, have given railroad intermodal marketing departments another chance to solicit household goods traffic. In its simplest form, intermodal movement of household goods means putting a moving van on a flatcar rather than on the Interstate, and several major moving companies (Mayflower, for example) have experimented with piggyback to some degree.

There is actually a long history of containerization of household goods. Many domestic moves are handled in semi-standard crates, which can also serve as storage units. Virtually all international household goods moves are containerized. In particular, the household belongings of US military personnel have been transported in containers of one kind or another for decades. The line-haul portion of a household goods move is really no different than any other freight movement, except for the great sensitivity to loss-and-damage. Articulated inter-modal cars, especially doublestacks, have for the first time enabled the railroads to offer a linehaul ride quality equal to or better than trucks, and the linehaul economics of intermodal transportation can make the railroads formidable competitors, especially for the growing num-ber of household moves arranged by corporate traffic departments.

Containerization of domestic liquid bulk commodities is opening up another new market opportunity for intermodal service providers. It is already underway with Union Pacific's "BulkTainer" service. As of 1989, UP had 42 BulkTainer service points where specialized local drayage was available to receive and deliver UP's fleet of nearly 200 tank containers. The IMO Type 1 tank containers, leased primarily from Sea Containers and Eurocontainers, vary in capacity from 5,300 to 6,600 gallons, and are lined and equipped to handle either food products (notably wine) or chemicals (including some hazardous materials). UP has under contract some 80 specialized low-boy chassis in place at its service centers. Loaded tanks are not yet permitted on doublestack cars (due to FRA regulations), but the service has grown despite this handicap. Other US firms, notably Chemical Leaman Tank Lines and Matlack, have been active in promoting and experimenting with domestic tank containers.

The domestic use of tank containers is likely to grow, just as their use has expanded within Europe and in international trade. The size and "go-anywhere" flexibility of tank containers fit in well with the trend toward smaller shipments and just-in-time logistics. Tank containers provide a chance for intermodal carriers to reach industrial shippers and consignees who do not have rail facilities or the traffic volume to justify full-sized railroad tank cars.

Traffic in set-up autos is another intriguing possibility that is being actively pursued. Three basic approaches are under development: removable auto racks for containers, piggyback trailers with hydraulic ramps, and auto-loading RoadRailers®. The primary goal is not linehaul cost savings, since roughly four intermodal units are required to equal one trilevel auto rack. Rather, the objectives are to extend the railroads' marketing reach and to reduce shipment damage.

Railroads now handle respectable shares of the factory-to-distribution center movement of new domestic autos, and of the port-to-distribution center movement of imports. If an intermodal system can be joined with precise production and inventory control, intermodal carriers have a chance to participate in the whole factory-to-dealer or port-to-dealer movement. A particular attraction of an intermodal system is the potential saving of intermodal transfer and local drayage over drive-on transfer and haul-away trucking.

The potential for damage reduction is also there, but intermodal equipment has yet to establish a track record despite some individual successes. Initial experiments and marketing efforts have focused on specialized, low-volume imports, including luxury cars. The general consensus within the industry is that intermodal transportation of set-up autos has a future. Whether autos become a major source of intermodal traffic, however, depends as much or more on the ability and incentives of the auto industry to exploit intermodal flexibility as it depends on equipment design or railroad marketing.

The future of refrigerated intermodal container traffic faces a stumbling block. For some years, refrigerated trailers have been a major source of piggyback traffic, carrying all manner of perishable goods, especially fresh fruits and vegetables. On the ocean and in port, refrigerated containers are a familiar sight. Yet domestic refrigerated piggyback has not been converted to containers, and international refrigerated containers have rarely ventured inland by rail. There are many reasons, but chief among them is the difficulty of supplying electrical power to container refrigeration units on board a train. Some "self-contained" refrigerated containers have refrigeration units built in, but require an external source of electrical power.

Aboard ship and in port, such containers are placed in special "reefer slots" where power is available. If a refrigerated container is to travel very far by highway, the chassis must be equipped with a "genset," a combination diesel engine and generator, to provide power. Refrigerated trailers are truly self-contained, having generator sets and refrigeration units mounted either on the front of the trailer (nose-mount) or underneath (belly-mount). None of these methods are suitable for rail cars, especially not for doublestacks. APL had some of its early stack cars equipped with large diesel generator sets to power doublestacked refrigerated containers, but has not so equipped any of its newer cars. Amtrak and other passenger carriers use "head-end power" from the locomotive to supply passenger cars with electricity, but freight locomotives and freight cars do not have that capability.

Containers with built-in gensets have been proposed, and some built, but the cost, service, weight, and cubic capacity penalties can be substantial. Although refrigerated piggyback is well-established, the future of refrigerated container movements by rail awaits either a technological breakthrough or a large-scale commitment to what is now an awkward and imperfect technology.

An unglamorous, but potentially important intermodal commodity is municipal solid waste: household garbage. Compacted garbage, ash from incineration or cogeneration, and recycled products must all be transported somewhere for burial, landfill or other disposal. The situation has become acute in many large metropolitan regions as the volume of garbage grows and the distance to acceptable disposal sites increases. Often, however, neither the central collection points nor the disposal sites are served by rail. Intermodal service, using either specialized or standard containers, may provide part of the solution. Many different schemes have been proposed, and some tested. One key question still to be answered is whether the outbound movement could ever be balanced by inbound traffic. If not, the costs of empty return may limit the potential of intermodal.

ISO Standards for a "Wide-Body" Container

Efficient intermodal operations depend on the right kind of equipment being available. For this reason, the development of a truly multi-modal container standard (i.e., not only marine) has become a major priority for the industry. However, with little real consensus emerging from recent meetings of ISO TC 104 Working Group 4 (WG #4, the ISO group charged with developing container standards), the prospects look remote for reaching agreement on a standard for the so-called "wide-body" container.

With new equipment types and sizes emerging in various domestic and international markets, the ongoing efforts of WG 4 to develop a standard for the wide-body container have come very much under the spotlight. The desire to reach agreement on a standard for future designs of container equipment has been voiced on both sides of the Atlantic, perhaps largely as a response to what some observers view as the "irresponsible" approach being taken by individual commercial concerns.

In the US, where domestic containerization is now poised to fulfill the promises of more than decade, increasing numbers of non-ISO units are finding their way onto the railroads and highways. Meanwhile, the utility of containers which conform to existing ISO dimensions is also being threatened by the development of a road/rail transportation system in Europe based on the swop body unit. ISO experts and commercial interests alike are suddenly anxious to standardize matters before they get out of hand.

In the Far East, the prevailing view may be one of desperation. In those countries where it is only comparatively recently that the 40-foot container was even allowed to operate at all, the prospects for widespread use of containers which exceed the present ISO maximum appear bleak. Nevertheless, even the Japanese have recognized that to participate in the standards process, however reluctantly, at least provides an opportunity to change the direction of the seemingly inexorable march toward bigger boxes.

At previous WG 4 meetings held in 1987 and 1988 there was wide consensus shown for the 102.36 inch (2.6

meter) width and the 9ft-6 inch high (2.9 meter) dimensions of the wide body container, which have already been adopted by TC 104. However, the width issue has been raised again with a suggestion that 2.591 meters may be politically preferable in Europe. Although the most recent working draft standard retains the 102.36 inch width, it has been agreed upon by WG 4 members that the matter should be discussed further at future meetings.

The most critical dimensional issue however, focuses on the length of the future wide-body containers, and agreement is clearly a long way off. WG 4 has been unable to reach agreement on ideal lengths, and academic, political and commercial motives continue to fuel the length debate.

For example, as a starting point WG 4 decided to adopt a methodology based on compatibility with standard pallet or unit load sizes. The ISO standard 1,200mm x 1,200mm pallet was chosen because it is the largest used anywhere. Controversy over this issue has never really been resolved, however, because pallets, which are generally constructed of wood, are prone to damage and rarely conform to strict dimensional criteria. Providing for the possibility of the "overhang" involved when cargo is palletized complicated the issue yet further. This led to the suggestion that the standard should provide for a "tolerance" or allowance for cargo which protrudes beyond the actual pallet dimension. The contradictions involved in calculating container length from a precise pallet size in tandem with an arbitrary "tolerance factor" presumably proved too much for some WG 4 experts, who concluded that a standard based on "zero-tolerance" was the only consistent approach.

Another key issue is the question of modularity. Does the international transportation community require a length dimension which can be halved, and in which the half-size enjoys the same efficiencies in terms of pallet use? Calculations show, for example, that a 40-foot long wide-body container is efficient for 1,200mm x 1,200mm pallets, accommodating ten double rows with 27mm tolerance for overhang. The half-size, the 20-foot unit, because of the extra wall space required, becomes very inefficient, however. No clear consensus has emerged with regard to modularity, although the majority view is that it is important.

Academic, political and commercial motives aside, problems of unit load compatibility and modularity are perhaps less severe than the obvious difficulties raised in the US where 45-foot and 48-foot containers have already achieved acceptance as the basis for a domestic container system. Despite the strong support from American interests for US domestic container lengths, the somewhat surprising outcome of the 1989 WG 4 meeting was that, based on a 1,200mm x 1,200mm standard unit load, voting finally came out in favor of two alternative approaches to an ideal length dimension. One approach is modular, 48-foot, 6 7/8 inches (14,805mm) and its half size 24-foot, 2 inches (7,365mm), and the other approach is a stand-alone maximum length of 40 feet (12,192mm). Ironically the 40-foot dimension received the most positive votes of the several put forward as candidates. Other than from the US experts, there has been little or no support for either a 45-foot or 48-foot length, let alone the 49-foot/24-foot, 5 inch (14,935mm/7,442mm) modular couple which appeared to have emerged as the favored size at WG 4's meeting in 1988.

Hopes that a specific resolution would emerge from the 1989 WG 4 meeting failed to materialize, however. Study of ideal lengths, based on other standard unit load sizes, is to continue at future WG 4 meetings, but it could be years before any real agreement can be reached on larger box sizes.

The diversity of the arguments on these issues raises many questions about the effort to develop a standard for a future wide-body container. For example, some experts have raised the threshold question as to whether this is really is the appropriate time to be seeking a standard at all. In fact, one of the group's major contributors was quoted as saying, "It is probably premature to have a standard right now." Others seem to take the view that the standards process should follow commercial usage and that ISO efforts are misguided.

The unit-load approach might also be questioned. Despite agreement to move forward with the analysis of other unit-load dimensions, it was pointed out that in excess of 50 pallet sizes were known to be in use around the world. The likelihood of one standard being able to accommodate all unit loads seems remote indeed. It is hard to escape the impression that the standards process has, rightly or wrongly, been taken over by politics and the professional academic, rather than being guided by legitimate commercial interests. It remains to be seem which approach will prevail, but a standard for the wide-body container still appears to be a distant goal.

Is There a Future for Piggyback?

Although five years of spectacular growth in inter-modal container traffic have not yet eliminated piggyback traffic, is there any reason to believe that piggyback service will endure? Without question, containers have a lower linehaul cost. Furthermore, their former stumbling block of chassis logistics and less cubic capacity are rapidly being reduced, if not eliminated. Many piggyback shipments have already been diverted to containers in the drive to balance the movement of international containers. In fact, one rail carrier has plans under which it might convert its entire intermodal traffic to containers by the early 1990s.

Santa Fe and Trailer Train, on the other hand, have invested heavily in new trailer-carrying capacity – Santa Fe with articulated Impack Cars and Trailer Train with all-purpose Spine Cars. Major leasing companies such as Strick, XTRA and Transamerica are replacing or rebuilding their trailer fleets, albeit at a rate short of expansion. Not all new technology is for containers either, such as the Trailer-Rail system which, as the name implies, is designed primarily for trailers. And although Canadian Pacific has containerized, Canadian National, the other major rail carrier in Canada, has retained its trailer service.

The largest single piggyback shipper, United Parcel Service, has yet to make any significant move toward containers. LTL truck lines, which have become important intermodal participants, are investing in 28-foot "pup" trailers rather than containers. Even American President still moves a substantial volume of trailer traffic via its third-party subsidiary, American President Distribution Services.

Thus, there is every indication that piggyback will remain a significant part of intermodal transportation for some years to come. As explained earlier, piggyback railers are still the only practical means for refrigerated intermodal transport. And even though the remaining intermodal hubs are being mechanized, effective chassis supply is still difficult in low-volume locations. Piggyback railers now being built or refurbished will probably still be active at the turn of the century. As appealing as a container-only system might be to intermodal purists, a pragmatic approach to intermodal will most likely include a place for trailer piggyback over at least the next decade.

Is There a Future for Carless Technologies?

In the mid-1980s, when RoadRailer® experiments were short-lived, many observers felt that carless technology was too "different" to survive in the railroad industry. With the more recent success of the Norfolk Southern Triple Crown service and CSX's Xpress Railer, it appears that the obituaries for carless technology were premature. Moreover, Norfolk Southern is expanding its Triple Crown service and successfully marketing carless technology to move a variety of commodities for both third-parties and shippers.

Numerous observers have tried to define a niche for carless technology. It is generally thought that carless trains are more suited to short hauls, in the vicinity of 500 miles, than to the transcontinental moves tacitly awarded to stack trains. Yet there is no inherent mileage limit to carless technology. BN and Gunderson have recently advanced the development of a specialized hitch for coupling RoadRailers® to stack cars, which may, in a single stroke, end the requirement for separate Road-Railer® trains and encourage larger RoadRailer® moves.

The minimal technical requirements for carless technologies, typically just a gravel surface surrounding the track, have been promoted as a means for carless technology to penetrate small markets that stack trains cannot. Carless technologies might therefore bring inter-modal service back to the myriad small piggyback ramps closed when hub-and-spoke operations began. One promising possibility is that major shippers can have their own carless facilities, and avoid the hub-and-spoke dray-age costs without investing in mechanical lift equipment. It remains to be seen, however, whether small volumes can support the service frequency required to compete with motor carriers.

Most likely, carless technologies will carve out their own niche, and it will be different from what has been predicted – just as carless technology is different from all that has come before.

Networks and Multi-modals

Conventional wisdom holds that the growth of inter-modal has been retarded by the lack of a national system. Intermodal service in the US has been called "bal-kanized". Each railroad may offer good service over its own routes, but rail customers have had to make their own arrangements for multiline trips. In recent years, this problem has been reduced by the use of runthrough trains and Voluntary Coordination Agreements.

Runthrough agreements allow trains to remain intact through interchange points, and when they work well, allow railroads to provide nearly "seamless" service over longer routes. The best runthrough arrangements, such as the UP-CNW interchange at Fremont, Neb., are all but invisible to the customers. Indeed, many casual

276

eferences are made to UP's "Los Angeles-Chicago" ervice despite the fact that nearly all such moves are nterchanged with CNW.

Voluntary Coordination Agreements (VCAs) can exend the advantages of coordination to the marketing and ales functions. Typically, VCAs provide for coordinated narketing over major interline routes, often where there s a single-line competitor. Burlington Northern has been . pioneer in the field, having negotiated VCAs with both irand Trunk Western and Santa Fe. The agreement with ianta Fe is in two parts, the second explicitly covering ntermodal marketing between the Southeast and South-vest. Both parties are thus engaged in marketing joint iN/ATSF service between points such as Memphis and .os Angeles, where neither can provide service alone.

Runthrough trains and VCAs can only take the ailroads so far, however, and have not yet provided either i national network of coordinated intermodal services or 'one-stop shopping" for intermodal transportation. The ;rowth of commercial and industrial shippers with nation-il distribution networks has increased the demand – and he opportunity – for intermodal networks to match. The eplacement of the regulated tariff system with a dere-;ulated contract system leads shippers and third-parties o rationalize their transportation purchases, dealing and legotiating with a smaller number of carriers to obtain :ustomized service. Customers would like to access a lational intermodal network with a single phone call, and :over their intermodal shipping needs with a single :ontract.

The national intermodal network is on the way. In act, in the future, intermodal customers will likely be ible to choose between competing national networks, just

277

as they choose long-distance phone companies. The phone-company comparison is apt, because the national intermodal networks are being created by multimodal companies extending their own services over a pre-existing infrastructure. As explained in Chapter 6, multimodals such as APC, BN America, and CSLI may or may not own railroads, steamship companies, motor carriers or intermodal equipment. The key feature is that they offer services as though they did. The long-distance phone caller need not know or care whether his call is routed over wires, fiber optics or microwave, or who owns the equipment, as long as the call goes through. The long-distance phone companies compete on end-to-end performance and price, and the multimodal companies do the same for intermodal transportation.

APC has gone the furthest in this regard. APC's subsidiary, American President Intermodal, offers a national system of scheduled intermodal trains, with API's own train symbols. API's train LK-5 is shown as running from Los Angeles and San Diego to South Kearny, N.J. In fact, cars assigned to API travel from Los Angeles to Chicago via Union Pacific and Chicago & North Western, and Chicago to South Kearny via Conrail. The San Diego containers are trucked in to Los Angeles. In any given week, API train LK-5 may be a dedicated doublestack train or a mixed train with business from other UP customers. The train may add or lose cars in North Platte or Chicago, if need be, and may not look quite the same from one week to the next. The customer, however, gets service from Los Angeles to South Kearny. In the same phone call, that customer can get service from Oakland to Atlanta, from Kansas City to Seattle, and from Detroit to Dallas.

CSLI's own network is growing, through additions to

its core of services on CSX and its Sea-Land trains under contract with western railroads for domestic services. Indeed, as of early 1989, CSLI and API were offering competing services between Southern California and the Southeast, a corridor in which neither company owns the infrastructure.

BN America was created not to own equipment or infrastructure, but to provide services over the BN system and extend them via contract to other railroads. BN America could eventually compete with API and CSLI in the Southern corridor.

These three multimodals, each starting from a different base, are building competing intermodal networks. All three intend to offer one-stop shopping for nationwide intermodal service. The services they provide will form an overlay to the national rail system. From the perspective of individual railroads, multimodals will be purchasers of contract services, which are then marketed under a common national nameplate.

So the nationwide network is coming – perhaps three competing networks for customers to choose from. Will there be other entrants, other nationwide networks? Although commercial success is notoriously hard to predict, there will doubtless be other attempts, and there is no reason why one or more should not succeed. Two attempts have already been made to run third-party RoadRailer® services over the railroads, one regional and one national. Interdom is loading stack cars in Iowa for domestic contract service on a small scale, and is considering expansion.

There is no fundamental reason why a nationwide intermodal network could not be built by one of the larger shipper's agents, since such third parties typically have multiple offices and terminals and contract service agreements with several railroads. The equipment leasing companies could pursue national contract services as a means to boost utilization of their equipment or as a way to add value to the low-margin leasing business. It is even conceivable that a major motor carrier, such as one of the nationwide LTL or high-service truckload firms, could add intermodal container services to its offerings. The nation's largest private handler of package freight, United Parcel Service, has been one of the railroad industry's largest intermodal customers.

Not only will there be national intermodal networks, but they will not be hamstrung by infrastructure. The same conventional wisdom that lamented the lack of a national network often held that the lack of infrastructure under common ownership could not be overcome – it was just too big and risky for any single company to pursue, and joint ventures were doomed to failure. The coming of the contract, the invention of the neutral chassis pool, and the flexibility of the equipment leasing companies changed all that. Risk is being reduced by contracting for only the services and equipment required for short-term growth, with the ability to scale up or down after a year or two.

The ability of Trailer Train to order stack cars for assigned service has contributed to the development of doublestack services by reducing risk. Railroads requested assigned cars based on volume contracts signed with customers (usually ocean carriers), and Trailer Train ordered cars based on railroad requests and commitments. The 1989 ICC decision prohibiting Trailer Train from assigning cars in this manner may be a handicap until or unless some other method is developed to share the risk.

Nonetheless, the intermodal industry has demonstrated convincingly that equipment and infrastructure ownership is not a prerequisite. More and more it is becoming apparent that the critical elements are management and marketing – everything else can be leased or purchased under contract. APC, CSLI and BN America are building their networks that way, and the future is open to other creative approaches for serving the intermodal customer.

Final Comment - the Political Issues

As far as the broad political issues surrounding intermodal transportation are concerned, there are signs of frustration, if not growing resentment, among intermodal executives. The fear is that the benefits of intermodal freight transportation are being ignored by legislators and bureaucrats too responsive to the special interests of one mode or another, and too little concerned with making strategic (and sometimes politically difficult) decisions about how the nation's freight transportation systems are going to operate in the future.

The fact is, despite the tremendous growth of intermodalism over the past five years, no political platform has yet been developed for the industry. With the US Department of Transportation divided into different sections, each representing the concerns of one mode of transport or another, the development of the marine, rail and highway industries is conceived of separately. The legislative process has become one of satisfying special transportation interests. And in this environment, the intermodal business has been without a voice. While rail and ocean carriers, railcar manufacturers and lessors have plunged headlong into marketing intermodal services and technology, behind the scenes little or nothing has been done to "cover the political bases." The industry has so far failed to develop a political presence.

A new type of transportation personality is now emerging, however: the "intermodalist." The term does not simply refer to someone involved in intermodal transportation. He or she is an intermodal protagonist – somebody willing to promote intermodalism and its technology at the public level, someone who sees intermodalism as an answer to the chronic problems facing the North American infrastructure.

These intermodalists are now beginning to speak out, particularly in the context of "Transportation 20/20," a program initiated in 1988 by the American Association of State Highway and Transportation Officials (AASHTO) and described as an "intensive multi-year effort to identify urgent highway and transit needs through the year 2020." Transportation 20/20's main goal is to develop a national consensus on future national surface transportation policy. At issue is the road infrastructure. With the Highway Trust Fund expiring in 1991, a major effort has been launched by an impressive coalition of highway interests in a massive effort to gain significant productivity improvements for motor carriers. The key questions are: will these highway interests compete or cooperate with intermodal interests? And, how will scarce federal and state funds be divided?

Without a doubt, the American Trucking Associations would have legislators spend all the funds available on state and federal highway improvements. ATA is publicly promoting a program that would continue the Highway

Trust Fund for highway improvements, refurbishment of bridges, research into better pavement design, and a relaxation of the 80,000-pound maximum gross weight restrictions. Predictably, the ATA also wants to exclude the possibility of the motor-carrier sector footing the bill for all this. Truckers are not interested in paying fuel taxes, weight or distance taxes, or tolls. Nor do they like the "time-of-day restrictions" being introduced in several urban port areas to relieve congestion during peak hours. The ATA and the trucking industry, by implication, are not primarily interested in intermodal logistics.

Meanwhile, intermodal advocates claim that multi-modal approaches to land transportation allow the shipper to take advantage of the best of both road and rail systems. But the argument extends beyond the mere marketing element. Maintaining a national surface transportation system means that planners need to consider how to optimize the *combined* transportation resources available. And this must mean intermodal solutions.

Further, intermodal transportation also promises to relieve environmental problems. 1985 statistics indicate that traffic on 61% of all urban interstate highways moves at speeds below 35 mph during peak hours. Added to this congestion, air pollution caused by trucks and cars compounds the issue. Intermodal, by making greater use of the railroad, presents at least a partial solution to the pressing environmental concerns that city and state transit planners are being forced to confront.

Additional economic arguments in favor of intermodal logistics include the view that doublestack, used for long-haul freight transportation, will relieve the pressure on the rural interstate highway system, allowing funds to be directed to the urban roads that need them most. Put another way, the sensible emphasis in a policy geared toward the optimization of the national infrastructure calls for an increased reliance on railway tracks so that local highway improvements and maintenance can be funded. This is not an argument the long-haul trucker wants to hear. But it may be the only direction a national policy can take.

Intermodal terminals and equipment also have an impact on the infrastructure. The on-dock transfer facility, at least where port space is available, gives carriers the ability to move containers from ships onto railcars within the marine terminal, so that enormous volumes of freight need not get onto the port area highways.

The arguments are persuasive. Yet few of these viewpoints are being cogently articulated and rarely are they being heard in the right places. For example, the way the US Department of Transportation has recently crafted new marine chassis inspection rules provides ample evidence of a lack of consideration of the intermodal argument. The new rules require that every commercial vehicle over 10,000 pounds maximum gross weight be inspected by a qualified mechanic at least once a year. Each vehicle must also carry with it a copy of the inspection certificate signed by the mechanic. Significantly, the regular Equipment Interchange Receipt (EIR) used in container depots and marine and rail terminals will not be sufficient to meet the requirements – a separate inspection must be carried out.

Clearly, in this instance, little consideration was given by DOT to the peculiar operating characteristics of the railroad, steamship line, equipment leasing and depot industries (in other words, all the intermodal players).

The intermodal viewpoint was either ignored or (more likely) simply not identified.

The most pressing difficulty, then, is that few legislators even know about intermodalism. To many legislators, intermodal means "taking the bus to the subway." Few have knowledge of ICTFs, doublestack railcars, post-panamax ships or the ramifications of the 48-foot container.

For this reason it is appropriate to end a book about "the intermodal revolution" with the suggestion that intermodal's destiny may be a function of the extent to which intermodalists get involved in the political process, and in particular, assist in shaping a national transportation policy which will govern growth in all carrier sectors for the remainder of this century and well into the next. As special interests maneuver for federal and state money, the reality is that non-intermodal protagonists carry the most political influence. Intermodalists need to develop more clout and involve themselves not only in intermodal marketing but also in intermodal politics.

This much is clear: funding for transportation projects over the next 10 years will be limited. Neither the shipper nor the carrier will benefit if the political imagination of legislators fails to rise above the kind of protracted and directionless battles between modal interests which have characterized past transportation policy making. Intermodal solutions may be obvious to the intermodalist. But it lies in the hands of the industry itself to make it apparent to federal transportation planners that multimodal approaches are the best means of meeting the environmental, logistic and cost efficiency requirements of a future national transportation policy.

INDEX